Kitchen Passport

FEED YOUR WANDERLUST WITH **85 RECIPES** FROM A TRAVELING FOODIE

ARSENY KNAIFEL

Creator of My Name is Andong

Kitchen Passport

FEED YOUR WANDERLUST WITH **85 RECIPES** FROM A TRAVELING FOODIE

For my mom,
who taught me how to eat

Publisher Mike Sanders
Senior Editor Ann Barton
Art Director William Thomas
Senior Designer Jessica Lee
Production Manager Grace Phan-Nguyen
Culinary Producer Kilian Peters
Photographers Eypee Kaamiño, Vic Harster
Food Stylists Diana Quach, Jana Wegner, Sissi Chen, Anna Knaifel
Recipe Tester Lovoni Walker
Proofreaders Lisa Starnes, Monica Stone
Indexer Celia McCoy

First American Edition, 2023
Published in the United States by DK Publishing
6081 E. 82nd Street, Indianapolis, IN 46250

Library of Congress Catalog Number: 2022941347
ISBN 978-0-7440-6609-8

DK books are available at special discounts when purchased in
bulk for sales promotions, premiums, fund-raising, or educational
use. For details, contact: SpecialSales@dk.com

Printed and bound in China

Cover and photographs on pages 5, 9, 251 © Vic Harster
All other images © Eypee Kaamiño

For the curious
www.dk.com

MIX
Paper | Supporting
responsible forestry
www.fsc.org   FSC® C018179

This book was made with Forest
Stewardship Council ™ certified
paper - one small step in DK's
commitment to a sustainable future.
For more information go to
www.dk.com/our-green-pledge

Contents

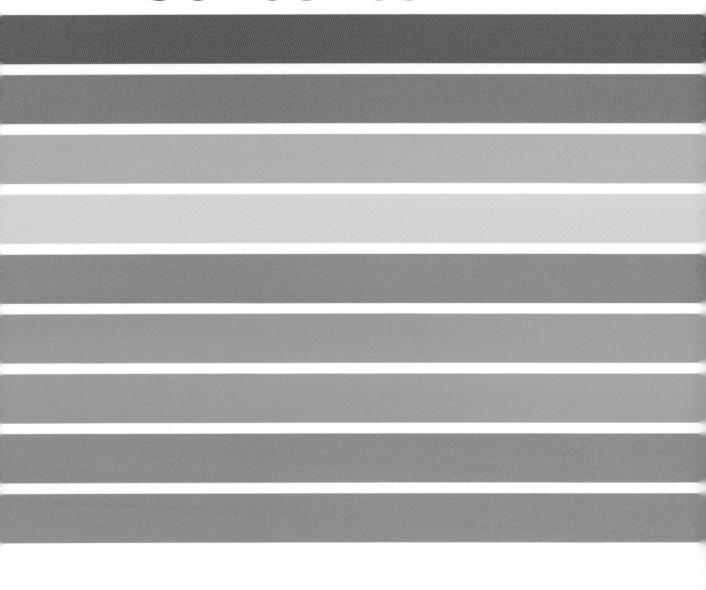

16   BREAKFAST

38   SOUPS

60   DUMPLINGS

90   STREET FOOD

118   MIDDAY MEALS

146   SALADS

172   DINNER

198   SAUCES AND CONDIMENTS

228   DRINKS AND DESSERTS

Introduction

What's your favorite part about traveling? If you are holding this book in your hands, chances are we have the same preference: we travel for food.

It hasn't always been like that for me. I used to get out a map and plan my itinerary according to the sights and places I wanted to visit. My meals were afterthoughts and would have to be planned around my itinerary; sometimes a sloppily packed sandwich and a banana would do.

Over time, I did a full one-eighty. When I travel now, I look at food recommendations first. I will walk across entire cities to get to remote locations, get up early for the best breakfast spot in town, and queue for hours to grab iconic street food. If there is time in between to see some epic architectural monument, fine, I'll do it (if there's a good bakery nearby). The reason is not simply that I want to taste the food—it's the whole experience of discovering it. And over time, I found yet another, even more passionate goal of mine: capture these moments of culinary adventure, get inspired by them, and find ways to re-create the moments I've had along the way.

If there is one person I have to thank for my outlook on food, it is the late Anthony Bourdain. The first time I saw an episode of his TV show on a random longhaul-flight, I was simply blown away by how skillfully he used food to shape a narrative around a region's cultural essence and the human condition in general. That was when I decided to follow a similar path: I want to tell stories about the world and the people living in it through the lens of food—stories not just about what we eat, but about why we eat it and how we came to do so.

After spending over five years filming videos about food, some more ambitious than others, I am excited to present to you a collection of recipes, stories, and inspirations that I accumulated over the first few decades of my life as a self-proclaimed traveling foodie. There are a few things you should know, though.

AUTHENTICITY IS A MYTH

The more time I spend researching and re-creating food, the more I realize that many foodies spend a lot of energy on chasing "authenticity." A fool's errand, if you ask me.

Food has always been a living, breathing thing. We can see this historically as recipes adapt to the state of the world, to cultural and societal trends, to natural events and human migration. Just because someone's grandma added a particular ingredient or you had it a certain way on your trip to Phuket back in 2002 does not make it more or less authentic.

I was once tasked with compiling a list of typical Berlin food. I guess people expected old-school German cooking, but instead the list featured dishes with Turkish or Vietnamese roots. Many people confronted me about it, but I firmly stood my ground. Most Berliners of my generation simply do not eat old-school German food on a daily basis. Köfte kebabs, pho, or pizza, on the other hand, end up on the menu weekly. But those are just newly introduced international foods, my critics would point out snarkily. To which all I can say is that even the humble potato— a staple of German cuisine, undisputed by even the most hardcore traditionalists— was a novelty from the far-off Kingdom of Peru less than two centuries ago.

The only definition of "authenticity" I will accept is this: it's what people *really* eat. Nothing else matters.

EXPECT THE UNEXPECTED

With that out of the way, what can you expect to find in this book? Elaborate, meticulously reconstructed recipes? Not quite.

It's not that it wouldn't be possible to re-create street food and home-cooking classics from around the world somewhat successfully at home. It's just that it would be a lot of work, and yet it would be missing the point. Even if you went through all the trouble of sourcing exotic ingredients and gathering highly specialized tools, in my view, you'd still not be able to live up to the original. It wouldn't be your fault—it's just that slurping a bowl of noodles from a plastic bowl while sitting on a tiny stool in a Taiwanese night market with all its sounds and smells will never be the same as doing so in your home kitchen. But that doesn't have to be a bad thing!

Instead, I am trying to find nuggets of inspiration within the eating experiences I've had around the world. Is there a certain technique, a philosophy, a flavor combination, or a presentation style that we can learn from and repurpose?

For the most part, the recipes I have developed for this book are just that: simple demonstrations of a cooking concept worth drawing inspiration from. Some stay fairly close to the traditional recipes they are meant to resemble, and some are wild, almost heretic interpretations.

Next to travel-inspired recipes, I will also not pass up this opportunity to introduce you to a few classics from German and Russian/Soviet cuisine, which shaped me in major ways as I was growing up.

COME FOR THE RECIPE, STAY FOR THE STORY

I always emphasize the value of storytelling in food, whether it's one of the countless incredible food origin stories I like to feature on my channel or a personal memory or experience associated with a certain dish or flavor.

This is why, embedded into each chapter, you will find a little essay or story inspired by my own food travels. Many of those will reference my time in China. It's not that I prefer Chinese cuisine to others (although sometimes, I might). It's just that Chinese culture used to be completely foreign to me, but the years I spent studying, working, and living there made it something of a home away from home. Without a doubt, food was my catalyst to learning about China, a means of bonding with local friends, and my ticket to understanding a whole new culture. It could have been any other country—it's more of a testament to the power of food as a social lubricant.

ONE FINAL NOTE

If you look at the ingredient lists in this book, you will quickly notice that I liberally recommend using MSG in home cooking. If this bothers you, relax. I am not a scientist, so I will not try to convince you to stop worrying about using small amounts of MSG in home cooking. Feel free to replace it with chicken bouillon powder (which itself probably contains MSG), use a 1:1 mix of sugar and salt, or leave it out entirely. I personally find it to be a fantastic shortcut for home cooks who don't have all day. My golden rule: don't use MSG to make bad food taste good; use MSG to make good food taste even better.

With all of these things out of the way—if you're ready—let me take you on a culinary journey around the world!

Essential Tools

There are a few kitchen tools I absolutely could not live without. Let me share some common classics as well as hidden champions you should have at hand.

Kitchen Scale

This is not optional. If you are serious about cooking (*especially* if you like following recipes), there is no way around getting a kitchen scale. I would even recommend getting two: a regular scale for most weighing tasks as well as a small precision scale for measuring things like salt or yeast down to a tenth of a gram.

Knives

I don't have to tell you how important a knife is in the kitchen. My personal collection is quite large, but the types I end up using the most are always the same: a large, heavy Chinese-style cleaver; a medium-sized chef's knife or santoku knife; and a small but chunky paring knife. With these three, you will be able to get nearly everything done in the kitchen.

Dough Scraper

Great for scraping dough, even greater for picking up chopped veggies and transporting them into their designated cooking or storing vessels.

Kitchen Scissors

Picked this up in Korea: sometimes the smartest choice when you need a knife is a pair of scissors. Try cutting garnish scallions or cilantro leaves straight onto your food with scissors and enjoy the satisfaction of being ahead of the curve.

Mortar and Pestle

An absolute must for grinding spices and creating pastes.

Silicone Spatulas

I got a set of differently shaped silicone spatulas because I'd seen high-end chefs use them, and it didn't take long to understand why they do. Just be sure to not leave them on a scorching hot pan for too long!

Straining Utensils

If you think about it, half of cooking is infusing oils and liquids with flavor and straining out the solids. A good set of sturdy fine-mesh stainless steel sieves as well as a slotted spoon and a spider will go a long way in the kitchen.

Kitchen Torch

Whenever you need a targeted little blast of heat to crisp up a crust or char an aromatic, the torch is your best friend—especially if, like me, you live in a place where gas stoves are not as common.

Cutting Boards

Choosing the right cutting board can have a tremendous impact on your cooking experience. I recommend having at least one *giant* all-purpose cutting board. It should be large enough to comfortably handle a watermelon, so don't skimp. You will also want at least one antibacterial plastic cutting board you can pop in the dishwasher and use as a designated meat board. Last but not least, have a small cutting board dedicated to garlic and onions (because there is nothing as frustrating as biting into a garlic-scented piece of freshly cut fruit).

Grater

Do yourself the favor and get a good-quality box grater as well as a rasp-style Microplane grater. They will come in handy more often than you'd think!

Large Bowls

Life's too short for small bowls. I have two enormous mixing bowls, one glass and one stainless steel, both of which are among the most-used items in my kitchen. The feeling of mixing or tossing things in them without worrying about spillover is one of life's great pleasures to me.

Wok

If you can only have one cooking vessel, it should be a wok. You can stir-fry, deep fry, boil, or steam food all in one. I'd recommend a flat-bottom wok, which I've always found a bit more convenient for home cooks, even if you have a gas burner.

Bamboo Steamer

Steaming might be one of the most underrated cooking techniques these days. It's convenient and efficient, and bamboo steamers look way cool. Choose a large one, but make sure you have a pot or wok it can fit into snugly.

Pantry

Whole cookbooks can be filled with smart advice on how to fill your pantry. With the right plan in mind, you could live from those ingredients alone for years. But aside from grains and canned goods, here is a list of super convenient items you will always find in my pantry and that have all come to my rescue many times during spontaneous cookouts.

Cornstarch

Great for dusting things (and unlike flour, doesn't clump or hydrate), making dredges for frying, or thickening liquids.

Clarified Butter / Ghee

Whenever you want that butter aroma but none of the burnt milk solids, clarified butter is your friend. Also a game changer for fans of homemade popcorn.

Mayonnaise

I always have an emergency tub of mayo in the back of my pantry. Mix it with literally any seasoning for a sinful but efficient dip, or use it as a base for marinades!

Tahini

Another shelf-stable hero. Can be mixed with water to form a thick and pasty sauce or more water for a thinner, lighter nutty dip. It's fantastic with both sweet and savory ingredients!

Garlic Powder and Onion Powder

Not just for the times when you're too lazy to mince garlic. These powders are like a light version of their fresh originals, with much of the bite removed. Sometimes that's not what you want, but sometimes that's exactly what you want. Mixed in sauces, dried garlic will add a mild but noticeable aroma that stays that way, rather than becoming overpowering like its fresh counterpart.

Dried Citrus Zest

I've cut my knuckles way too many times while attempting to zest overpriced, untreated lemons. Then I discovered dried zest, which does a fantastic job—especially for cakes and cookies.

Spice Blends

You probably have a whole drawer full of spices that you should use way more often. But there are three spice blends I always like to have around because they are shortcuts to flavor profiles that I strongly associate with particular cuisines. Five spice powder is my "instant Chinese;" curry powder or garam masala my "instant Indian;" and harissa, *ras el hanut,* or even taco seasoning my "instant Middle Eastern." Of course these overgeneralizations are not even remotely doing these great cuisines justice, but they are handy assets for a quick midweek meal.

Instant Coffee

Not just for when you run out of coffee: a tiny bit of this can enhance many dishes. Baking anything with chocolate flavor? Add a bit of instant coffee powder. Making a rich chili con carne? Add coffee! Sounds crazy, but it adds an instant nutty note.

Milk Powder

I don't have any tricks up my sleeve when it comes to milk powder, but I can't tell you how many morning coffee or baking sessions were saved by the pack I have in my pantry.

Agave Syrup

For whenever you want to sweeten things but you aren't sure if sugar would dissolve well. Agave syrup also has a slightly caramelly note, making it really tasty.

Citric Acid

Like the opposite of agave syrup, citric acid is a great tool to increase acidity without adding liquid.

Toasted Sesame Seeds

I can only recommend getting a jar at the store or making your own. Add them to a salt shaker with large holes to make your life a lot easier!

Breakfast

What better way to start this cooking journey than with breakfast! Discovering different local breakfast traditions is one of the travel experiences I most look forward to. My reaction to the new cooking styles, ingredients, and flavors I encounter usually lands somewhere between "Where have you been all my life?" and "This shouldn't taste so good at 8 in the morning!" The recipes in this chapter comprise some of my favorite breakfast discoveries. I hope they bring the same joy to your mornings.

Chicken Congee **21**

Youtiao **23**

Black Bean Ful Medames **24**

Chilaquiles **27**

Pandesal **31**

Chechebsa **33**

Blini **35**

Jian Bing **37**

Breakfast: A Traveler's Delight

Which flavor will set the mood for the day? Do I want to keep it light or load up on energy? As the first big food decision of the day, breakfast is unique. I hope this selection of recipes will spark both comfort and a sense of adventure in you.

CHINESE BREAKFAST

I have Russian roots, so the concept of porridge for breakfast is certainly not new to me. In fact, buckwheat, millet, and oat porridges were so ubiquitous on my family visits that I quickly lost interest in the sugared and buttered bowls of mushy grains.

I carried this attitude toward all types of porridge deep within me. When I lived in China, I resisted trying *zhou* for months. Zhou, often called *congee* or *rice porridge* in English, is a breakfast staple in many parts of the country, but the thought of a thin, most often rice-based paste didn't exactly get me excited. One day, I was stranded overnight in a small Chinese town and decided to give it a shot, due to a lack of options in the early morning as I was waiting for my bus—and my mind was blown.

Zhou turned out to be a perfect vehicle for flavor. Its smooth texture and mellow taste won't overpower you in the morning, but the pangs of flavor provided by the add-ins you choose will wake up your flavor buds in no time. Start with my **chicken congee,** but don't hesitate to play around with condiments and toppings!

If you're feeling brave, you might even want to slice up a **youtiao** and add that**.** This cruller has made its way around Asia and is also a common sight in Thailand or Vietnam. If you make some, be sure to try them with a cold glass of lightly sweetened soy milk.

One of my favorite ways to eat youtiao is stuffed inside a **jian bing** (Chinese breakfast crepe) as a decadent breakfast upgrade. Though admittedly, jian bing is more often stuffed with another type of deep-fried dough, a crispy cracker. Either way, this eggy, savory crepe with many layers of texture is one hell of a contender to a classic Western breakfast sandwich.

THE DOUBLE LIFE OF FLATBREAD

Every once in a while, I remind myself to go for a completely different style of breakfast. I find it important to not get overly used to one type of food and keep an open mind. What could be better than starting the day with a little adventure?

When I'm in the mood for Mexican food but I simply can't justify a big burrito this early in the day, I like to go for **chilaquiles.** The idea of soaking tortilla chips in sauce is simply genius and a great way to use up stale leftovers—as well as a reminder that many of the world's most beloved dishes are born out of necessity or limitation.

Thousands of miles from Central America, Ethiopians are enjoying **chechebsa,** which shares a few similarities with chilaquiles, for breakfast. A large flatbread is prepared, only to be torn up and tossed in infused butter and the region's signature spice mix. I was once served this with eggs and honey and still dream about it. To speed up the process, I often make chechebsa with store-bought flatbread.

BRINGING IT BACK HOME

Not far from my studio in Berlin, there is a neighborhood I like to call Little Beirut. One of the best parts is the fantastic Levantine food. Starting early in the morning, the scents of hummus, lemons, and cheesy flatbreads fill the air. When you take a peek inside the shops, you can see enormous pots with chickpeas and fava beans bubbling away.

For breakfast or an early lunch, I will go for **ful medames.** Eaten in North Africa and the Levant, this simple-but-hearty fava bean stew needs only a bit of spice, lemon, and olive oil. Even though this is best made with fresh beans soaked overnight and cooked for hours, I find using canned beans more than reasonable at home. It was my insatiable urge to experiment that led me to try it with black beans (my favorite beans!), and I was surprised by how well it worked. As long as you respect the origins of a dish, I see nothing wrong with having it your way.

I could never leave you without a bread recipe in a breakfast chapter. I have definitely baked my fair share of loaves. Which, to be honest, is a little absurd when you live in Germany, one of the world's most bread-obsessed countries—not just in terms of bread eaten per capita but also in terms of variety. German bread can be white as a cloud and dark as a . . . pumpernickel. And yet, the one bread I think beats them all for breakfast is a **Filipino pandesal,** a heavenly soft, buttery and sweet roll that only gets better when sandwiching a thick piece of butter and maybe a bit of cheese. Paired with a good cup of coffee or milk tea, this might even beat a croissant for me.

In the end though, no matter how many incredible food discoveries I might still make in the future, the one breakfast that will forever have a special place in my heart is my Babushka Enna's **Russian blini.** A lot of Eastern Europeans enjoy them with sour cream and jam—which is delicious—but my grandma always makes them ahead of time, stuffed with cheese and dill, and reheats them. For me, no breakfast tastes more like home.

CHICKEN CONGEE

SERVES
2-3

PREP TIME
10 minutes

COOK TIME
65 minutes

If you are unsure about porridge, this recipe might very well change your mind. This comforting, Chinese-style rice congee is as good for brunch or breakfast as it is for a miracle pick-me-up for the next time you're feeling under the weather!

DIRECTIONS

1. In a medium pot, bring the water to a boil over medium-high heat. Stir in the salt and rice, then add the chicken. When the water has come to a boil again, cover, reduce the heat to medium-low, and simmer for 15 minutes.

2. Remove the chicken and set aside. Cover the pot with a lid, and continue to simmer the rice for another 30 to 40 minutes or until the grains of rice have burst and the liquid has thickened significantly.

3. Meanwhile, when the chicken is cool enough to handle, shred it with two forks or your hands.

4. When the congee has finished cooking, remove it from the heat, and stir in the shredded chicken, oyster sauce, sugar, and MSG. Divide evenly among 2 to 3 serving bowls. Add toppings to each bowl, as desired.

5 cups **water**

½ tsp **salt** (or more to taste)

½ cup **jasmine rice,** thoroughly rinsed

½ **chicken breast** (5oz / 150g)

1 tbsp **oyster sauce**

1 tsp **granulated sugar**

¼ tsp **MSG**

FOR TOPPING (OPTIONAL)

3 tbsp chopped **preserved Chinese mustard greens**

1-inch (2.5cm) piece **fresh ginger,** finely julienned

2 **scallions,** green parts only, finely sliced

2 tbsp chopped **fresh cilantro,** packed

2-3 tbsp **soy sauce**

2-3 tbsp **dark Chinese vinegar**

2-3 tbsp **Chili Crisp** (page 204)

1-2 tsp **toasted sesame oil**

1 tsp **ground white pepper**

YOUTIAO
(CHINESE BREAKFAST CRULLER)

MAKES
6–8 youtiao

PREP TIME
30 minutes + 4 hours to rest dough

COOK TIME
15 minutes

This cruller is sometimes dubbed "Chinese doughnut," but I disagree with that description—it is so much more. The simplest way to enjoy youtiao is by simply dipping it in lightly sweetened soy milk for breakfast. But try it as a side dish for meaty broths like pho, and prepare to have your mind blown!

2½ cups **all-purpose flour** (12.3oz / 350g)

1 tbsp **baking powder** (0.4oz / 12g)

½ tsp **baking soda** (0.1oz / 4g)

½ tsp **salt** (0.11oz / 3g)

1 cup cold **whole milk** (8oz / 250g)

2½ tbsp **neutral cooking oil** (1oz / 30g), divided, plus more for greasing

8–10 cups **vegetable oill**, for frying

Soy milk (optional), to serve

DIRECTIONS

1. In a medium bowl, combine the flour, baking powder, baking soda, salt, milk, and 1½ tablespoons cooking oil. Mix until the dough is just combined, and cover the bowl with a damp towel or plastic wrap. Rest for 15 minutes.

2. Knead the dough for 5 minutes and shape it into a rough rectangle. Grease the rectangle with some of the remaining cooking oil, and place it into a large zip-top bag. Add the remaining 1 tablespoon cooking oil, squeeze most of the air out of the bag, and rest on the counter for 4 hours.

3. Lightly oil your work surface. Remove the dough from the bag, and roll it into a long rectangle roughly ¼ inch (0.5cm) thick and 4 inches (10cm) wide. Cut the dough into strips about 1 inch (2.5cm) wide.

4. Stack two strips on top of each other. Briefly dip a chopstick in water, then place it along the middle of the double strip lengthwise and press the two halves together firmly. They should stick together in the middle, creating a butterfly-like cross section. Repeat the process until no more strips of dough remain.

5. Fill a deep fryer or large Dutch oven about two-thirds full with vegetable oil and heat to 375°F (200°C). Holding an assembled youtiao by its two ends, gently shake to stretch it by about an inch or two. (It should still comfortably fit into your fryer.) Carefully place the stretched dough into the hot oil. Using cooking chopsticks, immediately begin to flip the frying dough until it is evenly cooked, puffed up, and golden brown. This should take about 2 minutes. Remove and place on a wire rack to drain the excess oil. Repeat for the remaining youtiao.

6. Serve the youtiao warm alongside a cold glass of good-quality, lightly sweetened soy milk for dipping, if desired.

BLACK BEAN
FUL MEDAMES

SERVES
3-4

PREP TIME
10 minutes

COOK TIME
10 minutes

Ful medames, a staple across many regions of the Middle East and Northern Africa, is one of the most nutritionally wholesome dishes I actually enjoy eating. It makes for a filling breakfast, and it's also a perfect hangover meal (but don't quote me on that). This version calls for black beans instead of the traditional fava beans, and I love it!

½ clove **garlic,** grated

Juice of 2 **lemons**

2 15oz (425g) cans **black beans,** drained and rinsed

1¼ cups **water,** divided

¼ tsp **ground cumin**

¼ tsp **kosher salt** (or to taste)

⅛ tsp **MSG**

½ tsp **smoked paprika**

4 tbsp **extra virgin olive oil,** divided

2 medium **tomatoes,** diced

½ **green bell pepper,** finely diced

¼ cup chopped **fresh parsley**

Fresh **pita bread** (optional), to serve

DIRECTIONS

1. In a small bowl, combine the garlic and lemon juice. Mix until combined. Set aside.

2. In a large, heavy skillet over medium heat, combine the black beans, ¾ cup water, cumin, salt, MSG, and smoked paprika. Bring to a low simmer and cook, stirring occasionally, for 5 minutes or until the water is almost fully evaporated. Remove the pan from the heat.

3. Stir in 2 tablespoons olive oil and the remaining ½ cup water. Using a potato masher, roughly mash the beans in the skillet. (About a third of the beans should remain intact.)

4. Transfer to serving plates and drizzle with the lemon-garlic sauce and remaining 2 tablespoons olive oil. Top with tomatoes, green pepper, and parsley. Serve with fresh pita bread, if desired.

CHILAQUILES
(MEXICAN BREAKFAST NACHOS)

SERVES
2

PREP TIME
10 minutes

COOK TIME
15 minutes

When I first heard of this dish, which is best described as "soggy nachos," I thought, *This is where I draw the line.* Until I tried it. Now it's a breakfast staple for me, especially whenever I have a sad bag of stale tortilla chips lying around.

DIRECTIONS

1. In a small bowl, combine the harissa paste, tomato paste, taco seasoning, water, and MSG. Set aside.

2. In a large skillet, heat the oil over medium-high heat until it shimmers. Crack in both eggs and fry for 2 minutes on the first side, then gently flip. Sprinkle with salt and fry for 15 seconds before turning the eggs over onto a plate. Set the eggs aside. (There should be some residual oil left in the skillet.)

3. In the same skillet, sauté the onion over medium-high heat for 2 to 3 minutes, stirring occasionally, until lightly caramelized. Reduce the heat to medium. Add the harissa mixture and bring it to a boil. When boiling, add the tortilla chips and mix until just combined with the sauce.

4. Transfer to a serving plate and top with the fried eggs, crumbled feta cheese, sliced radishes, avocado, and cilantro.

NOTE: You can go for any type of tortilla chips you like. I prefer them plain, but make sure to taste for saltiness. Some brands might come fully unseasoned, in which case you can add ¼ teaspoon salt to your sauce.

2 tbsp **harissa paste**

1 tbsp **tomato paste**

1 tbsp **taco seasoning**

1 cup **water**

¼ tsp **MSG** or **fish sauce** (optional)

2 tbsp **neutral cooking oil**

2 large **eggs**

⅛ tsp **salt**

1 small **onion**, finely diced

3½ oz (100g) **tortilla chips** (see note)

TO SERVE

2 oz (50g) **feta cheese** or **queso fresco**, crumbled

2 **radishes**, thinly sliced

¼–½ **avocado**, cubed

2 tbsp chopped **fresh cilantro**

What makes good breakfast? It might depend on where you are.

The sun had just appeared behind the Andean mountains on a cool October morning. It was day two of my long-awaited journey to the Amazon rainforest, and a sense of adventure was fueling my appetite. I followed my nose to the little kitchen of a slightly rundown brick guesthouse, curious what I'd get to try for breakfast. Thanks to its geography, Peru is a country with a fascinating food culture. Fresh seafood from the coast, beautiful potatoes of all colors from the Andean mountains, and a variety of exotic fruits grown in the tropical climate of the Amazon have helped the nation become home to some of the world's most inspired chefs.

To my disappointment, that morning's breakfast consisted of greasy, lukewarm scrambled eggs and stale white bread that had traveled with us in a plastic bag, accompanied by margarine and neon-red strawberry jam. Don't get me wrong— we were in a small Andean village; I did not expect a five-star brunch. But the warm smell that had gently awoken me that morning certainly didn't come from these offerings. As I obediently started slurping up my eggs and considering the off-brand Nutella I'd discovered at the other end of the table, I glanced over to my tour guide. Aptly named Darwin, he was an upbeat and experienced Quechua rainforest guide with a strong physique. He was sitting at a small table separate from the rest of the group, chatting with the driver. In front of them were big bowls of rice topped with mounds of saucy pale purple beans, their hot steam shimmering in the morning sun. I was immediately struck with envy. This was what I had smelled earlier and hoped to get to eat myself. Too shy to ask, I finished my breakfast in silence, secretly sighing at every whiff of the rice and beans one table over.

Later that day, I sneakily asked my guide why he wasn't having breakfast with us. "We are giving you the good stuff," Darwin answered. "We were having a local dish, rice with beans and some Andean greens. Tourists usually don't like it, so we bring their breakfast along and only the crew eats the guesthouse food." How wrong he was, I thought—but I was still too shy to verbalize it. "So do you think Western breakfast is the good stuff?" I asked instead. "No way," he laughed. "I don't like it. But you guys aren't used to our type of food, especially in the morning."

Hearing this was way more disappointing than it should have been. But I had my reasons. In my mind, every single meal, especially in a place new to me, is also an opportunity to experience something unexpected and literally get a taste of another culture. Just like getting some exercise in the morning can boost your energy for the day, going on a little culinary adventure sets you up for a day of exploration.

I thought back to my first bowl of *mohinga*, the national breakfast of Myanmar. Sold by street vendors and in tea houses across the country, it's a savory, mildly spicy, almost curried rice noodle soup. Between catfish, banana stem, lemongrass, toasted chickpea flour, and dozens of other ingredients, it could not be further from what I used to have for breakfast growing up. And yet it was love at first sip.

While living in China, I sometimes enjoyed organ meat, fried dough, and fermented tofu curds for breakfast. When I told my friends about breakfast favorites like these I had encountered on my travels, I was occasionally met with disbelief. "How can you eat something like that for breakfast?" some would ask. But I have never understood why we have these arbitrary rules about what is and isn't appropriate for breakfast.

These rules and boundaries are everywhere; you don't even have to look far. I grew up in Germany, where it is not uncommon to have cheese and cold cuts on rustic rye bread for breakfast. One country over in France, the idea of having anything other than sweet foods for breakfast will seem wild to many. I have often wondered why Americans seem to find it completely appropriate to have what is essentially a burger for breakfast, as long as the patty is made from "breakfast sausage." And while most of us would also never order a pizza for breakfast, it's common wisdom that leftover pizza makes for an excellent morning meal.

In the end, no food is inherently suited or unsuited for breakfast. It's all about habit. And once we give our own breakfast habits some thought, we might find that other countries' "unusual" breakfast choices may not be so undesirable after all—in fact, they may be exceptionally tasty.

On my third day of the trip, as we traveled down from the Andes into the transitional area between the mountains and the jungle called a cloud forest, I enjoyed a delicious bowl of rice and beans for breakfast.

PANDESAL
(FILIPINO SWEET MILK BUNS)

MAKES
12 buns

PREP TIME
25 minutes + 2 hours to rise

COOK TIME
30 minutes

If you like bread, you will love pandesal. The heavenly soft texture and lightly sweet flavor of these luxurious rolls pair perfectly with a generous pat of butter, a little cheese, and a cup of instant coffee. (Yes, I said instant coffee!)

DIRECTIONS

1. In a small saucepan, combine ½ cup whole milk and 2 tablespoons bread flour. Whisking constantly, heat over medium heat for 1 to 2 minutes or until fully thickened. Remove from the heat and let cool for at least 10 minutes.

2. Meanwhile, in a medium bowl, combine the remaining ¾ cup milk, egg, and melted butter.

3. In the bowl of a stand mixer, combine the remaining bread flour, milk powder, sugar, salt, and yeast. Whisk until combined.

4. To the bowl of the stand mixer, add the wet ingredients and cooled flour paste. Using the dough hook attachment, knead for 2 minutes on low and 10 minutes on medium-high. The dough will be quite wet but should come together into a shaggy ball. Add a small amount of additional flour, if needed.

5. Transfer to a lightly greased large bowl, cover, and place in the oven with just the light on to rise for 1 hour or until doubled in size.

6. Punch down the dough and divide in 12 equal-sized portions (roughly 2 ounces or just under 60 grams each).

7. Line a baking sheet with parchment paper. Place the bread crumbs in a medium bowl and fill a second bowl with room temperature water.

8. Shape each piece of dough into a taut ball. Working one by one, drop each ball into the bowl of room temperature water. Using a spoon, lift the ball out and let excess water drip off completely before transferring to the bowl of bread crumbs. Gently toss and roll around until fully coated.

9. Evenly space out the breaded balls on the prepared baking sheet and loosely cover with plastic wrap. Proof on the counter for 45 minutes or until doubled in size and plump.

10. Preheat the oven to 450°F (230°C). Remove the plastic wrap, and place the baking sheet into the oven (middle rack). After 3 minutes, lower the heat to 370°F (180°C). Bake for 20 to 30 minutes or until golden and the internal temperature registers 200°F (93°C). Cool on a wire rack for 5 minutes. Pandesal are best eaten warm but can be stored in an airtight container for up to 3 days after fully cooling.

1¼ cups cold **whole milk**
(10fl oz / 300ml), divided

2¾ cups **bread flour**
(12.3oz / 350g), divided

1 large **egg**

4 tbsp **unsalted butter**
(2.1oz / 60g), melted

2 tbsp **milk powder**
(0.5oz / 15g)

5 tbsp **granulated sugar**
(2.3oz / 65g)

1 tsp **salt** (0.25oz / 7g)

1 packet **instant yeast**
(0.25oz / 7g)

1 cup **bread crumbs**
(1.8oz / 50g)

CHECHEBSA
(ETHIOPIAN SPICED HONEY FLATBREAD)

SERVES
1-2

PREP TIME
5 minutes

COOK TIME
15 minutes

This simple yet highly satisfying breakfast dish is very popular in Ethiopia and with good reason: the rich, sweet, and spicy flavors come together beautifully to kick-start your day. This is a perfect opportunity to use your best honey!

DIRECTIONS

1. In a small pan over medium-low heat, warm the clarified butter until it is completely melted. Add the berbere spice and smoked paprika, and gently heat for 5 seconds or until fragrant.

2. To a medium bowl, add the flatbread and pour the spiced butter over it. Sprinkle with ⅛ teaspoon salt. Toss until all of the surfaces are coated, and set aside.

3. In a small bowl, whisk the eggs with a pinch of salt. In a wok, heat the oil over medium-high heat until it begins to shimmer. Add the eggs and cook undisturbed until big bubbles form. Roughly scramble into medium-sized curds. Set aside.

4. To the same wok, add the seasoned flatbread and cook until slightly crispy but still chewy and tender on the inside. Return the scrambled eggs to the pan and toss to mix.

5. Transfer to a serving plate. Top with yogurt, sliced chilies and cilantro (if using), smoked paprika, and honey. (Be generous with the honey drizzle!)

1 oz (35g) **clarified butter** or **ghee**

½ tbsp **berbere spice**

½ tsp **smoked paprika**

3½ oz (100g) fluffy **flatbread,** torn into bite-sized pieces

⅛ tsp + a pinch of **salt,** divided

2 large **eggs**

1 tbsp **neutral cooking oil**

TO SERVE

3 tbsp **plain Greek yogurt**

2 **green chilies** (optional), sliced, to garnish

2 sprigs **fresh cilantro** (optional), leaves only, roughly chopped

Pinch of **smoked paprika**

2 tbsp **honey** (0.9oz / 25g)

BLINI
(RUSSIAN PANCAKES)

MAKES
6–8 blini

PREP TIME
10 minutes + 30 minutes to rest dough

COOK TIME
20 minutes

No blini will ever come close to the ones my Grandma Enna makes for me every time I visit. That said, this recipe is approved by her, super quick, and guaranteed to satisfy both your sweet and savory crepe cravings—with a Russian twist!

DIRECTIONS

1. In a medium bowl, combine the eggs, oil, sugar, salt, and flour. Whisk until a smooth, thick batter with no lumps is achieved.

2. Combine the milk and water. Add to the batter one-third at a time, ensuring the liquid is fully incorporated before adding more. You should end up with a very thin, almost watery batter. Rest in the fridge for 30 minutes or overnight.

3. Over medium heat, preheat a 10-inch (25cm) nonstick skillet. Add 1 teaspoon clarified butter, and spread across the surface of the pan.

4. Holding the skillet off the heat, pour one ladle of batter (about ⅓ cup) and swirl around to form an even, crepe-like pancake. (If you get a few small holes, you can carefully patch them by adding a few drops of batter from a teaspoon.)

5. Cook for 1 to 2 minutes on the first side or until the top is no longer liquid, beads of oil begin to collect on the surface, and the edges begin to turn a crispy brown. With a spatula, check to see if the bottom is golden brown and flip the blin. Cook for 45 seconds more until a few golden-brown spots appear on the other side. Transfer the cooked blin to a plate and repeat with the remaining batter, coating the pan with about 1 teaspoon clarified butter between each blin.

6. Blini are ready to eat out of the pan and can be topped, filled, folded, or rolled to your desire. For traditional savory or sweet blini, let the entire batch cool for 20 to 30 minutes and proceed with the following steps.

7. **For sweet blini,** fold 4 blini in half and in half again. Using the same pan as before, melt ½ tablespoon clarified butter over medium-high heat. Add the 4 quartered blini. Crisp on both sides for about 1 minute. Serve with a dollop of cold sour cream and jam.

8. **For cheese-stuffed blini,** mix cheese, dill, chives, and pepper in a small bowl. Spead the filling over one side of a blin, then fold the blin in half and in half again. Using the same pan as before, melt ½ tablespoon clarified butter over medium-high heat. Add the quartered blin. With the lid on, warm on both sides for 1 to 2 minutes or until the exterior is crispy and the cheese has melted. Serve with a dollop of sour cream, if desired.

2 large **eggs**

2 tbsp **vegetable oil** (0.9g / 25g)

2 tbsp **granulated sugar** (1.4oz / 40g)

⅓ tsp **salt**

1¼ cups **all-purpose flour** (5.3oz / 150g)

¾ cup **whole milk** (5oz / 150g)

1½ cups **water** (10oz / 300g)

3 tbsp **clarified butter,** for cooking, divided

SWEET TOPPING (PER BLIN)
1 tbsp cold **sour cream**

½ tbsp **raspberry jam** or other jam

SAVORY FILLING (PER BLIN)
¼ cup **shredded cheese,** packed (young Cheddar or similar)

½ tbsp finely chopped **fresh dill** (optional)

½ tbsp minced **fresh chives** (optional)

½ tsp freshly cracked **black pepper** (10 cracks)

1 tbsp **sour cream** (optional)

JIAN BING
(CHINESE BREAKFAST CREPE)

MAKES
3 jian bing

PREP TIME
30 minutes

COOK TIME
15 minutes

I've always prefered savory crepes to sweet ones. When I first had jian bing, it sealed the deal. Saucy, crunchy, tender, spicy, and salty with every bite—it leaves little to desire. Even without the equipment traditionally used by street-food vendors, you can re-create this classic Chinese breakfast at home!

DIRECTIONS

1. To make the sauce, in a small bowl, combine all sauce ingredients. Mix until the fermented bean curd has been broken down into small chunks and the sauce achieves a spreadable consistency. Set the sauce aside.

2. In a medium bowl, combine the all-purpose flour, mung bean flour, salt, water, oil, and five spice powder. Mix until the batter is smooth and no lumps remain. Set aside to rest for at least 30 minutes or up to overnight in the fridge.

3. Meanwhile, make the cui bing crackers. In a medium saucepan, heat the cooking oil to 350°F (180°C) or until the oil bubbles rapidly when a wooden chopstick is inserted into the oil. Carefully place 1 wonton skin into the saucepan and cook on both sides for 30 seconds or until light golden-brown. Once cooked, place the fried wonton on a wire rack. Repeat with the remaining wonton skins. Allow the fried wontons to drain and to firm up for at least 5 minutes. Use right away or transfer to a zip-top bag and freeze for later use.

4. Into a cold, lightly greased large skillet, pour ½ cup of batter. Evenly spread the batter around the surface of the skillet. Place over medium heat and cook for 3 to 4 minutes or until the batter has just set on the surface.

5. Over the pancake, crack an egg, break the yolk, and spread the egg across the surface of the pancake with a spatula. Cook for 2 minutes, then loosen the pancake by slowly running the spatula beneath its edges.

6. Top the pancake with chopped cilantro and scallions, and flip. Spread a thin layer of sauce over the pancake, and sprinkle with preserved mustard stem and lightly crushed cui bing crackers.

7. Fold the pancake into a pocket by first overlapping two sides over the center, then folding it in half over itself. (This creates a perfect shape to be eaten from a sandwich bag.) Repeat with the remaining batter. Sprinkle with black sesame seeds (if using), and enjoy immediately.

NOTE: Mung bean flour can be hard to source but is available at some Asian grocery stores as well as online. It can be made at home by blending mung beans in a food processor for several minutes. Most flours will work as a substitute—try buckwheat, chickpea, or corn flour, or a blend of different types.

1⅓ cups **all-purpose flour** (5.3oz / 150g)

⅓ cup **mung bean flour** (not mung bean starch; see note) (2.6oz / 75g)

⅛ tsp **salt**

1¼ cups **water** (10oz / 350g)

1 tbsp **neutral cooking oil**

Small pinch of **five spice powder** (optional)

3 large **eggs**

2 tbsp finely chopped **fresh cilantro**

2 tbsp chopped **scallions**

2 tbsp finely chopped **preserved mustard stem** (also called zhacai, optional)

Black sesame seeds (optional)

FOR THE CUI BING CRACKERS

1½ cups **neutral cooking oil,** for deep-frying

20 frozen **wonton wrappers,** thawed

FOR THE SAUCE

2 tbsp **hoisin sauce**

1 tbsp **doubanjiang** (fermented chili bean paste)

1 tsp **red fermented bean curd** (optional)

1 tsp **granulated sugar**

Soups

No doubt about it: soup is one of the most common—if not *the* most common—forms of serving food around the world. Whether you're at high sea, setting up camp deep in the mountains, or strolling through a new trendy street-food market in a bustling metropolis, there's only one thing that's for sure: there will be soup.

Souped Up Borscht **44**

Svekolnik **45**

Grace's Canh Chua **47**

Laksa, Tom Kha Style **48**
  Easy Rempah **50**
  Shrimp Balls **51**

Lohikeitto **55**

West African Peanut Soup **56**

Turkish Lentil Soup **59**

Soup: the Ubiquitous Comfort Food

Although soup is wildly popular all over the globe, the methods, textures, and flavor profiles are anything but the same. Consider this chapter your sneak peek into the many forms of brothy goodness around the world.

For anyone growing up in a Russian family, soup is ubiquitous. Along with an appetizer, salad, and a main course of meat and grains or potatoes, it is one of the fixed courses that make up a traditional meal in this part of the world. This might be the root of my complicated relationship with soup: for the longest time, I took it for granted. And to be fair, Russian soups are often unglamorous—simply a practical means of feeding a family. At some point, I simply lost interest in what I came to consider the most boring of food categories.

It wasn't until one particularly cold winter day that I felt an intense craving for a steaming bowl of hearty soup deep inside of me. Not even half an hour later, I was at my go-to Turkish place, shoving spoonfuls of ultra-smooth and peppery mercimek çorbası (**Turkish lentil soup**) into my mouth and wondering why I had been missing out all those years.

This was the moment "Soup Season"—a favorite series on my channel—was born. It's an exploration of the fascinating world of soup, in the hope that nobody will ever take its comforting magic for granted again.

NEAR, FAR, WHEREVER YOU ARE

Remember my initial indifference toward Russian soups? Shockingly, they're still not my favorite. Often cabbage-laden, overpowered by too much bay leaf, and too thin in texture for my taste, I will still opt for something more exciting in texture, flavor, or both if given the choice. The notable exception is borscht, probably the most widely known of all Eastern European soups, thanks to its vibrant deep-purple color. I've given this classic soup a bit of an upgrade by incorporating a few umami-packed ingredients usually found in Asian cooking. This is the **borscht** recipe you will find in this chapter—one that I believe can win over even the harshest borscht critic.

There is another version of borscht I have always liked, even without adulteration: I'm talking about **summer borscht**. A well-known and quickly made Lithuanian variety of its famous cousin, summer borscht is made from fresh, uncooked vegetables and served cold. The addition of kefir or other sour dairy turns the color from a deep purple to a bright pink and adds extra tang, making this a very smart choice for hot summer days.

But let us take a step away from borscht and turn toward a completely different soup culture. When my channel producer Grace started working for me, we often ended up chatting about food that reminded her of home. As a Canadian-Vietnamese, her repertoire included everything from all-dressed potato chips to all things maple syrup to Westernized Vietnamese food, including this iteration of **canh chua**—a unique and super tangy soup. Even though many ingredients are hard to source outside of Vietnam, there is a ton you can learn from trying it. Let's just say if you thought pineapple on pizza was controversial, try this.

And since we're talking about Asian soups, there is no way of getting around **laksa**. Laksa is a whole family of noodle soups commonly found in Southeast Asia, and with the additions of intensely fragrant spices as well as rich coconut milk, it is almost in curry territory. The best part? The **shrimp balls** and **rempah** spice paste from this recipe freeze well and make for great cooking shortcuts.

A UNIVERSAL LANGUAGE

Soup has the extraordinary feature of being both a familiar sight in every part of the world as well as an educational insight into a region's food culture.

West African peanut soup is a great example of this. Who knew a jar of peanut butter could be a fantastic base for soup? Only people from one of the world's biggest peanut-producing regions could have come up with that, and I'm glad they did. If anyone ever says soup doesn't make them full, let's see what they say after a bowl of this.

And finally, we can come full circle and talk about **lohikeitto**. While it's originally from Finland, I had my first spoonful in the Russian-Finish border region of Karelia, where the main ingredients of salmon, cream, leek, and potato are abundant. Though I added a few extra twists to this rustic soup, its essence is in those base ingredients. Just another reminder that great food does not need to be fancy.

SOUPED UP BORSCHT

SERVES
5

PREP TIME
30 minutes

COOK TIME
4 hours

Most traditional Eastern European meals start with a soup, and the one soup to rule them all is borscht. I admit I was never a huge fan until I started tweaking the recipe. The unexpected secret ingredient? Kimchi! (Don't tell my grandma, please.)

DIRECTIONS

1. Preheat the oven to 400°F (200°C). Line a baking sheet with parchment paper. Quickly rinse the beets, wrap each one in foil, and place them on the prepared baking sheet. Bake for 60 minutes or until the beets are fork-tender. Rest beets for at least 20 minutes or until cool enough to handle. Peel off the skins and grate the beets into a bowl, making sure to keep both the flesh and the juice.

2. While the beets are roasting, fill a large stockpot with water and bring to a boil. Add the beef. As soon as the water comes back to a boil, cook for 15 seconds, and then remove the beef. Discard the cooking water and rinse the beef under cold water to remove foamy scum and impurities.

3. Return the beef to the stockpot, and add 8 cups water and salt. Bring to a boil. Add the peppercorns, bay leaves, allspice, coriander, ginger, and shiitake mushrooms. Reduce the heat to low, cover, and simmer for 2 to 4 hours. Add water as needed to keep the ingredients submerged.

4. In a medium skillet over medium-high heat, add the carrot, onion, and olive oil. Sauté for 5 minutes. Add the tomato paste and cook, stirring frequently, until the tomato paste is caramelized, about 2 minutes. Set aside.

5. Remove the beef from the pot, separate the meat from the bone (if necessary), and cut into bite-sized chunks. Strain the broth and return it to the pot.

6. Bring the broth back to a boil. Add the potatoes, cabbage, beets, cooked carrot and onion, kimchi, kimchi brine, caraway, sugar, vinegar, and MSG (if using). Cover and simmer over medium-low heat, stirring occasionally, for 30 minutes or until all veggies have fully softened. Stir in the grated garlic just before serving.

7. Serve in a large soup bowl, garnished with a large dollop of sour cream and dill. Highly recommended: eat this Ukrainian style with garlic bread on the side!

2 large **red beets**

2 lb (900g) **bone-in beef shank** or **chuck roast,** cut into large chunks

8 cups **water** (2L), plus more as needed

1 tsp **salt** (or to taste)

½ tsp **black peppercorns**

2 **bay leaves**

2 **allspice berries,** lightly crushed

1 tsp **coriander seeds**

5 slices **fresh ginger**

3 **dried shiitake mushrooms**

1 large **carrot,** grated

1 large **onion,** grated

3 tbsp **olive oil**

2 tbsp **tomato paste**

2 **waxy potatoes,** grated

⅛ head **green cabbage,** shredded

5 oz (150g) **kimchi,** thinly sliced

⅓ cup **kimchi brine** (3.5oz / 100g)

1 tsp **ground caraway**

1 tbsp **granulated sugar**

1 tbsp **white vinegar**

½ tsp **MSG** (optional)

1 clove **garlic,** freshly grated

Sour cream, to serve

Chopped **fresh dill,** to serve

SVEKOLNIK
(COLD SUMMER BORSCHT)

SERVES
4

PREP TIME
20 minutes

COOK TIME
5 minutes

I get it—nobody wants to eat a hearty stew in the middle of a hot summer day. This is why the babushkas of Eastern Europe came up with svekolnik—an irresistibly refreshing summer version of everyone's favorite Slavic soup. It doesn't hurt that it looks so pretty either!

DIRECTIONS

1. Bring a small pot of water to a boil over high heat. Reduce the heat to medium, add the potato, and cook for 5 minutes or until fork-tender. Let the potato cool, then finely dice.

2. Into a large bowl, grate the beets. Add the sour cream, vinegar, and pickle juice. Stir to combine. Add the radishes, potato, cucumber, pickle, scallions, dill, pepper, MSG, salt, sugar, and water. Stir gently to incorporate.

3. Serve immediately or—even better—refrigerate for 2 hours and enjoy cold. Garnish with dill and half of a hard-boiled egg, if desired.

NOTE: Traditionally, this recipe is made from young beets, but you can use any beet you can find. Precooked works just fine, but for extra flavor, get them raw and roast them, wrapped in foil, for 90 minutes at 350°F (180°C).

1 large **waxy potato**

5 medium **precooked beets** (about 20oz or 550g, see note)

14 oz (400g) **sour cream** (around 25% fat)

2 tbsp **white vinegar**

2 tbsp **pickle juice**

4 small **radishes,** finely diced

½ **cucumber,** finely diced

1 **dill pickle,** diced

2 **scallions,** finely chopped

2 tbsp chopped **fresh dill,** plus more to garnish

½ tsp freshly cracked **black pepper** (10 cracks)

½ tsp **MSG**

1 tsp **salt**

1 tbsp **granulated sugar**

2 cups **water** (16fl oz/ 500ml)

2 **hard-boiled eggs** (optional), to garnish

GRACE'S CANH CHUA
(VIETNAMESE SWEET & SOUR SOUP)

SERVES
3–4

PREP TIME
10 minutes

COOK TIME
15 minutes

I was introduced to this unusual but delicious soup by my lovely channel producer Grace. This recipe was developed with her guidance. She says: *Canh chua is one of my comfort foods and reminds me of home. The light, savory, tangy, and fresh broth make any bowl of plain rice the perfect decadent meal. This dish is usually paired with a peppery braised fish and fresh salad.*

DIRECTIONS

1. Dice 1 tomato and cut the remaining 2 tomatoes into wedges. Set aside.

2. In a medium pot, heat the oil over medium heat. Add the garlic and scallion whites. Gently sauté for 1 to 2 minutes or until the garlic is golden brown and the scallion whites are softened. Add the diced tomato and sauté until it has released its juices and completely softened.

3. Add the water, tamarind paste, sugar, bouillon powder, and fish sauce to the pot. Cover with a lid and bring to a boil. When boiling, add the shrimp, tomato wedges, zucchini, and pineapple. Reduce the heat to medium and simmer for 5 minutes, uncovered.

4. Remove from the heat, and stir in the Thai basil, scallion greens, and bean sprouts.

5. Serve over rice, if using, garnished with the sliced chili, cilantro, or more Thai basil. Add lime juice and fried shallots to taste.

NOTE: When purchasing tamarind paste, be sure to check the ingredients and choose one that contains 100 percent tamarind purée.

3 **tomatoes**

2 tbsp **neutral cooking oil**

4 cloves **garlic**, minced

2 **scallions**, white and green parts divided, chopped

6 cups **water** (1.5L)

2 tbsp **tamarind paste** (1.8oz / 50g, see note)

¼ cup **granulated sugar**

1 tbsp **chicken bouillon powder**

¼ cup **fish sauce** (60ml)

12 oz (340g) large **raw shrimp**, peeled and deveined

1 small **zucchini**, cut into bite-sized pieces

5 oz (140g) **canned pineapple**, cut into bite-sized pieces

4 sprigs **Thai basil**, plus more to garnish

3½ oz (100g) **bean sprouts**

TO SERVE
Steamed **white rice** (optional)

1 **fresh Thai red chili**, thinly sliced

Chopped **fresh cilantro**, to taste

Lime juice, to taste

Fried shallots (store-bought), to taste

LAKSA, TOM KHA STYLE

SERVES
3-4

PREP TIME
15 minutes

COOK TIME
20 minutes

As a kid, I loved tom kha soups from the local Thai place—who doesn't? About two decades later, I fell in love with laksa, a Malaysian rice noodle soup. Something inspired me to fuse them into one, and this recipe was born. The best part? The shrimp balls and spice paste can be used for many other dishes!

DIRECTIONS

1. Blanch the mung bean sprouts and bok choy by placing them in a large bowl and submerging them completely in hot water. Soak for 5 minutes, then drain and set aside.

2. To a medium stockpot, add the oil and rempah paste. Quickly stir and cook over medium-high heat for about 1 minute or until the paste becomes fragrant.

3. Add the dashi, lime zest, fish sauce, brown sugar, and coconut milk. Bring to a boil. When boiling, add the mushrooms, shrimp balls, and lime juice. Simmer for 5 minutes.

4. To serve, prewarm 3 to 4 serving bowls. Into each bowl, place a handful of noodles, bean sprouts, and bok choy. Ladle the soup over top and garnish as desired with cilantro or Thai basil and red chilies. Serve with lime wedges on the side.

2 generous handfuls of **mung bean sprouts**

2 heads **baby bok choy**, leaves cleaned and separated

2 tbsp **neutral cooking oil**

2½ tbsp **Rempah** (page 50) or **red curry paste**

3 cups **instant dashi stock** or **chicken bouillon** (24fl oz / 700ml)

1 **lime** (zest and juice, divided)

2 tbsp **fish sauce**

1 tbsp **brown sugar**

1 cup **coconut milk** (8fl oz / 250ml)

6 **button mushrooms**, quartered

8-12 **Shrimp Balls** (page 51)

7 oz (200g) **thin rice noodles**, cooked according to package instructions

TO SERVE (OPTIONAL)

Fresh cilantro or Thai basil

Fresh Thai red chilies

Lime wedges

EASY REMPAH
(RED CURRY PASTE)

SERVES
3–4

PREP TIME
5 minutes

COOK TIME
None

2 stalks **lemongrass,** white and pale green parts only, roughly chopped

1-inch (2.5cm) piece **fresh ginger,** peeled

3 cloves **garlic**

1 medium **shallot**

½ tbsp **tomato paste**

2 fresh Thai red chilies

½ tbsp **red chili flakes**

¼ tsp **salt**

3 tbsp cold **water,** plus more as needed

DIRECTIONS

1. To a food processor, add the lemongrass, ginger, garlic, shallot, tomato paste, Thai red chilies, chili flakes, and salt. Blend until combined. Add cold water 1 tablespoon at a time to achieve a smooth paste. Add up to 2 extra tablespoons of water if you have trouble processing the paste.

2. Use immediately or transfer to an ice cube tray and keep in the freezer for up to 3 months.

SHRIMP BALLS

SERVES
2-3

PREP TIME
10 minutes

COOK TIME
15 minutes

7 oz (200g) raw, semidefrosted **shrimp** (any size), peeled and deveined

10 oz (280g) boneless, skinless **chicken breast**

4 tsp **cornstarch**

1 tsp **salt**

1 tsp **granulated sugar**

¼ tsp **five spice powder**

¼ tsp **ground white pepper**

6-9 tsp **ice water**

DIRECTIONS

1. To a food processor, add the shrimp, chicken, cornstarch, salt, sugar, five spice powder, and pepper. Blend until homogenous. With the motor running, add the ice water 1 teaspoon at a time until a smooth, paste-like texture is achieved.

2. Prepare a large bowl with an ice water bath. Wet your hands and a teaspoon. Gently scoop a roughly egg-sized portion of the paste into the palm of your hand, and squeeze out a walnut-sized portion through the index finger and thumb. Scrape the blob with the spoon to shape it into a ball and drop it into the ice water bath. Continue until all the paste is used.

3. Fill a medium pot two-thirds full with water, and bring to a boil over medium-high heat. Carefully transfer the shrimp balls into the pot, and bring the water to a gentle simmer. As soon as it starts to bubble, reduce the heat to medium-low, and cook for 6 minutes while maintaining a low simmer.

4. Once cooked through, remove the shrimp balls with a strainer or slotted spoon, and place into an ice water bath for 5 minutes. Drain. Eat the shrimp balls immediately or keep in a zip-top bag in the freezer for up to 6 weeks.

Soup: an Ancient Concept for Modern Times

Soup has come a very, very long way in its roughly 20,000-year history. In fact, 20,000 years may be an understatement—this is just what the oldest soup bowls still in existence date back to. Soup as a concept might be older—maybe even much older. It might not even be of human origin! Or to be more precise, not of *Homo sapiens sapiens* origin. That's right—many historians are convinced it was the Neanderthals that brought us soup.

Needless to say, ancient soup makers were not using fancy induction burners. Instead, they utilized what might be the oldest cooking technique known to humanity (aside from roasting over open fire). They would dig a pit, line it with animal skin, and fill it with water. In the meantime, they'd have some rocks heating up in a fire. Once scorching hot, the ancient cook would drop the hot stones into the water, along with whatever edible plant and animal parts were available. *Et voilà,* proto-soup.

Why bother going through the trouble of cooking in a time before you could post food pics on social media? Quite simple, actually. Making proto-soup killed off harmful bacteria, unlocked nutrients, and made food last longer. Given enough time, even inedible items like tough roots, plant scraps, and bones could be turned into delicious broths. That extra availability of energy and nourishment is what allowed humans to start thinking about things other than mere survival. You could almost argue that soup is what made humans human in the first place.

This deeply rooted connection to soup has been with our species for millennia. Technological advancements like the inventions of pottery and metalworking further propelled the spread of soup making around the world, and we have never stopped loving it. The idea that you can make enough food for a family just by throwing whatever you have on hand into a pot with liquid is just too tempting.

Even in an increasingly industrialized world, people have never abandoned soup and instead continue to innovate around it.

Once we figured out canning, one of the first things to end up on kitchen shelves in this form was soup. A painting of a can of soup is even one of the world's most recognized works of art.

Once we got the hang of industrially dehydrating food for preservation, we immediately saw the opportunity to create powdered soups and bouillon cubes.

Even today, soup seems to be on the cutting edge of food trends. I'm talking about anything from bougie 38-hour broths that are sold for 10 bucks a cup to countless instant ramen recipes that keep hardworking students fed and focused.

But soup is by no means just a basic source of nutrition. Fine dining is obsessed with crystal clear consommés; some of Berlin's hottest food spots proudly display their pho master stocks, which seem to be bubbling away and slowly cooking beef into oblivion for days.

No question about it—soup is clearly still front and center when it comes to our eating habits, and it's here to stay. In fact, it was never not here. Maybe it is indeed the one food that makes us human more than any other.

LOHIKEITTO
(FINNISH CREAMY SALMON SOUP)

SERVES	4
PREP TIME	15 minutes
COOK TIME	30 minutes

While lohikeitto is a very common soup in Finland, I first had it in the Russian-Finish border region of Karelia. This recipe is a very liberal interpretation of this dish and an attempt to fuse it with some of my favorite flavors from Japanese and Southeast Asian cookery.

DIRECTIONS

1. In a medium bowl, combine the miso, cornstarch, fish sauce, and cream. Whisk until the cornstarch and miso have fully dissolved. Set aside.

2. Place the potatoes, carrot, and leek in a large pot. Add the water and salt. Bring to a boil over high heat, then lower the heat to medium-high and cook for 10 minutes. Remove the leeks and reduce the heat to medium.

3. Place the peppercorns, juniper berries, and bay leaves in a muslin spice bag. Add it to the pot and simmer for 10 minutes. Remove and discard the spices.

4. Add the salmon and cook for 3 to 4 minutes.

5. Whisk the miso slurry once more before adding it to the pot. Briefly let the soup come up to a simmer to thicken, and then remove the pot from the heat. Stir in the dill before serving.

3 tbsp **white miso** (1.8oz / 50g)

4 tbsp **cornstarch**

4 tsp **fish sauce**

¾ cup **heavy cream** (7oz / 200ml)

2 large **potatoes**, peeled and cut into 1-inch (2.5cm) cubes

1 large **carrot**, peeled and cut into 1-inch (2.5cm) cubes

½ **leek**, white and light green parts only, cut into 1-inch (2.5cm) segments

5 cups **water** (1.5L)

1 tsp **salt**

½ tsp crushed **black peppercorns**

3 **juniper berries**, crushed

2 **bay leaves**

7 oz (200g) skinless **salmon**, cut into bite-sized pieces

3 stalks **fresh dill**, leaves only, roughly chopped

WEST AFRICAN PEANUT SOUP

SERVES
4

PREP TIME
10 minutes

COOK TIME
25 minutes

You might be surprised to see almost an entire jar of peanut butter used to make a soup, but wait until you have experienced the luxurious texture it provides. If you ever questioned soup's ability to be a rich and filling meal, this West African–inspired recipe should settle things once and for all—and it's completely plant based, too.

DIRECTIONS

1. To a large pot on medium heat, add the oil, onion, and ginger. Cook, stirring occasionally, for 4 minutes or until the onion begins to caramelize. Stir in the tomato paste and berbere spice and toast for 1 minute.

2. Add the water, sweet potato, MSG, and soy sauce. Stir in the peanut butter and simmer on medium-low heat for 15 minutes, stirring occasionally, until the potato is tender.

3. Turn off the heat, stir in the spinach, and serve.

2 tbsp **neutral cooking oil**

1 large **onion**, diced

1 tbsp grated **fresh ginger**

2 tbsp **tomato paste**

1½ tsp **berbere spice** or **garam masala**

6 cups **water** (1.5L)

1 large **sweet potato**, diced

½ tsp **MSG**

¼ cup **soy sauce**

1 cup **creamy peanut butter** (9.5oz / 270g)

9 oz (250g) **frozen spinach**

TURKISH LENTIL SOUP

SERVES
4

PREP TIME
10 minutes

COOK TIME
40 minutes

Turkish food is ubiquitous in my hometown of Berlin. My number one rule: no matter what you order, get lentil soup on the side. Silky smooth, highly nutritious, and mild in flavor (but not in the least boring), it can be a meal on its own or an always-welcome upgrade. Divine with a dash of paprika oil and a squeeze of lemon!

DIRECTIONS

1. Place a medium stockpot over medium-high heat. Add the olive oil, butter, onion, and garlic. Sweat the aromatics for 2 to 3 minutes or until they begin to brown. Stir in the tomato paste, and cook for 2 minutes more or until lightly caramelized. Add the potato and lentils. Cook for 2 minutes more, stirring frequently, until fragrant.

2. Add the water, salt, and pepper. Cover and cook for 30 minutes, stirring occasionally to prevent burning at the bottom of the pot.

3. Meanwhile, prepare the paprika oil. In a small skillet, heat the oil until light wisps of smoke appear. Place both varieties of paprika in a small heatproof bowl, and pour the hot oil over them. Stir to combine and let sit for 10 minutes.

4. When the soup is done cooking, with an immersion blender, blend the soup until smooth. Stir in the dried mint and MSG. If the soup is too thick for your liking, add water, a few tablespoons at a time, to thin.

5. Garnish with chopped parsley and a swirl of paprika oil. Serve with lemon wedges on the side, if desired.

2 tbsp **olive oil**

2 tbsp **butter**

1 **yellow onion**, diced

3 cloves **garlic**, minced

1 tbsp **tomato paste**

1 **potato**, peeled and diced

1 cup **split red lentils**
(7oz / 200g)

4 cups **water** (1L)

1 tsp **salt** (or to taste)

½ tsp freshly cracked **black pepper** (15 cracks)

1 tsp **dried mint**

½ tsp **MSG**

FOR THE PAPRIKA OIL

¼ cup **neutral cooking oil**

1 tsp **paprika**

1 tsp **smoked paprika**

TO SERVE

Chopped **fresh parsley**

Lemon wedges (optional)

Dumplings

My definition of the term "dumpling" is quite liberal; you could debate whether some of the dishes in this chapter should even be classified as such. But if you let me, I'd like to take you on a holistic exploration of the concept in all its facets. Let's celebrate the diversity of dumplings!

Kuya Eypee's Lumpia **64**
    Pork & Shrimp Filling **67**
    Tofu & Mushroom Filling **67**

Jiaozi **68**
    Pork & Bok Choy Filling **71**
    Beef, Celery & Carrot Filling **71**

Bolivian Salteñas **72**
    Andean Green Salsa **74**

Sheng Jian Bao **76**

Oven-Baked Samosas **80**
    Uzbek-Style Beef Filling **82**
    Potato Masala Filling **82**

Pork & Shrimp Wontons with
  Chili Oil **85**

Momdong's Russian Pirozhki **86**
    Chicken Filling **89**
    Cabbage & Egg Filling **89**

Dumplings: the Universal Appeal of Stuffed Dough

It seems that every culture on this planet has their own favorite dumpling. Which immediately raises the question: what even is a dumpling?

Look at global food trends, and you'll see a pattern: a little nugget of a flavorful substance (often seasoned ground meat) is sealed in a mild-tasting starchy wrapper, briefly cooked, and served multiple pieces at a time. But a closer look will reveal that the world of dumplings is vast, and the devil is in the details here.

There are obvious differences in shape and fillings—and not all dumplings have fillings in the first place. Nor do all dumplings have wrappers, or fully enclose the filling. The wrappers can be crumbly, crisp, or chewy, and the cooking methods vary wildly. However, all the recipes in this chapter share the common thread of a pleasingly tidy package from somewhere around the world.

WORK YOUR WAY UP

If you are new to the world of homemade dumplings, the easiest way to get your feet wet is to start with a dumpling that uses store-bought wrappers. There is no shame in doing so. What determines whether you can skip the DIY wrapper and go industrial has less to do with flavor and more to do with its storability and textural consistency thereafter. Fortunately, a few of the world's favorite dumplings do exceptionally well in this scenario!

The easiest to work with, and my recommended gateway dumplings, are fried spring rolls. They are nearly foolproof to make, and even in China, making the ultrathin spring roll wrappers from scratch is practically unheard of. For this selection, I wanted to highlight **lumpia shanghai,** the Filipino cousin of the spring roll. (Not least as a nod to longtime channel videographer Eypee, who is half Filipino and who offered his expertise in developing this recipe.)

Once you get the hang of things, it's time to move a step up and try your hand at some **wontons.** They also do very well with store-bought wrappers, and the folding technique is very forgiving. While you will often find wontons floating in soup, I prefer serving them with a simple chili oil and soy sauce dressing, and I think you will too.

HARD WORK PAYS OFF

Once you have successfully mastered the store-bought wrapper, it's time to try making your own. It might seem intimidating at first, but you'll improve quickly with practice, and the results will speak for themselves. I recommend starting with **jiaozi,** a super classic Northern Chinese variety that is often generically referred to as "Chinese dumplings." The simple wheat flour wrappers will teach you all the basic skills you need to know. Pro tip: make a "hot water dough" by using boiling instead of regular water, which denatures the proteins in the flour and results in a very forgiving dough, perfect for beginners.

The next step will lead you to what I consider to be "the king of Chinese dumplings": **sheng jian bao.** The addition of yeast makes this a leavened wrapper, meaning the dough will rise and leave you with the most fluffy, tender love child of a *jiaozi* and a steamed *bao.* Speaking of steaming, sheng jian bao are steamed and panfried at the same time! Wild, I know.

But for all my love of Chinese dumplings, we also need to look beyond the Middle Kingdom. For example to the region just a little west: Central Asia. You have probably heard of Indian **samosa.** I love the traditional *masala* potato filling, my take on which I included in this chapter. But when it comes to preparation, I decided to go with a style I encountered while traveling in Uzbekistan: the oven-baked samosa. (Thank me later when you enjoy fresh samosas in a kitchen that will not smell of grease for days.)

SIZING IT UP

But since we are already entering the twilight zone between dumplings and hand pies, let's go all the way. On a trip to Latin America, I was delighted to discover the **Bolivian salteña.** These are baked and much larger than most dumplings I encountered in Asia, but the most notable differences are the filling and the almost crunchy baked crust.

Last but not least, I simply couldn't not share a recipe for **Russian pirozhki.** My mom has been making these forever, and hers are hard to beat. The good news is that she helped me with the recipe in this book, and we hope you will learn to love them. The wrapper is buttery, tender, and yeasty, and goes perfectly with my mom's chicken filling as well as a traditional vegetarian cabbage-and-egg base.

And speaking of fillings, of course you can mix and match the fillings from this chapter, and I encourage you to tweak them to your liking! Congratulations, friend—you have now scratched the surface when it comes to dumplings.

KUYA EYPEE'S LUMPIA
(FILIPINO-STYLE SPRING ROLLS)

SCAN FOR VIDEO

MAKES
25 lumpia

PREP TIME
30 minutes

COOK TIME
30 minutes

Most of us know spring rolls as a Chinese specialty, and they technically are. But while I've only encountered them a handful of times in China itself, the love my Filipino friends have for "lumpia Shanghai," their local rendition of this globally beloved snack, is beyond anything. Longtime channel videographer Eypee is an especially huge fan, so this recipe was developed with his help and approval!

25 10-inch (25cm) **spring roll wrappers,** fully defrosted

1 batch **Lumpia Filling** (page 67)

6–8 cups **vegetable oil,** for frying

DIRECTIONS

1. To wrap a lumpia, place a spring roll wrapper in the shape of a diamond on a work surface, one corner pointing up. (Scan QR code for video instruction.)

2. Place about 2 tablespoons of filling on the wrapper, about one-third of the way from the bottom corner. Using your hands or a spoon, form it into a short sausage-like shape.

3. Starting from the bottom, tightly roll the wrapper around the filling and halfway up the spring roll. Moisten your index finger with water and wet the two remaining unfolded top edges of the wrapper. Fold in the sides of the wrapper first, then tightly roll the filling all the way up.

4. Place the filled roll on a clean surface, seam side down. Repeat until no more filling remains.

5. In a deep fryer or large Dutch oven, heat the vegetable oil to 350°F (180°C). (If using a Dutch oven, fill two-thirds full with oil.)

6. Working in three batches, fry the spring rolls for 7 to 8 minutes per batch or until golden brown. Rest on a cooling rack for at least 5 minutes before eating. Serve with Kuya Rafa's Sawsawan Dip (page 215) or Sweet Chili Sauce (page 207) for dipping, if desired.

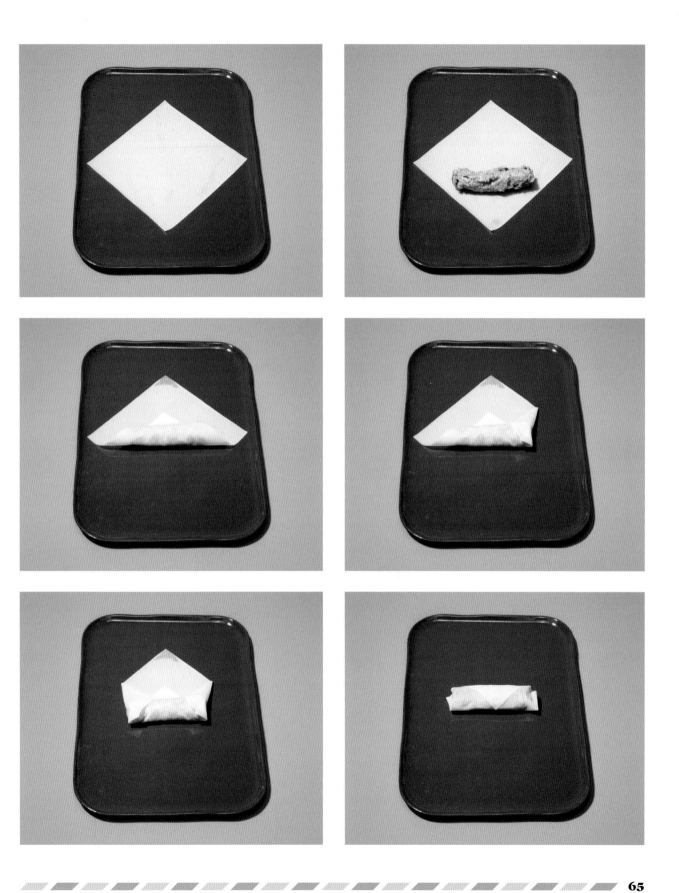

LUMPIA FILLING:
PORK & SHRIMP

MAKES
Filling for 20–25 lumpia

PREP TIME
15 minutes

DIRECTIONS

1. In a food processor, combine the pork, shrimp, onion, pepper, Maggi, salt, and cornstarch. Pulse for 1 to 2 minutes until a fine but not completely homogenous mass forms.

2. Transfer to a medium bowl. Add the cilantro, scallions, and carrots, and mix until fully incorporated. The mixture can be used immediately or refrigerated for up to 2 days before use.

1 lb (500g) **ground pork**

12 oz (350g) **frozen shrimp** (any size), thawed

1 **white onion**, roughly chopped

1½ tsp freshly cracked **black pepper** (50 cracks)

2 tbsp **Maggi seasoning** (or 1 tbsp soy sauce + 1 tbsp Worcestershire sauce)

1 tsp **salt**

1 tbsp **cornstarch**

½ cup finely chopped **fresh cilantro**

2 **scallions**, finely minced

2 medium **carrots**, finely grated

LUMPIA FILLING:
TOFU & MUSHROOM

MAKES
Filling for 20–25 lumpia

PREP TIME
15 minutes

DIRECTIONS

1. Rehydrate the mu-erh mushrooms by soaking in hot water for 20 minutes. Cook the glass noodles according to package instructions.

2. In a food processor, combine the tofu, mu-erh mushrooms, glass noodles, enoki mushrooms, onion, cornstarch, soy sauce, sesame oil, Maggi, and water. Pulse for 2 minutes until a fine and homogenous texture is achieved. (Alternatively, you can finely chop all ingredients by hand.)

3. Transfer the mixture to a large bowl. Add the cilantro and carrot, and mix until fully incorporated. The filling can be used immediately or refrigerated for up to 2 days before use.

1 oz (30g) **dried mu-erh** (wood ear) **mushrooms**

2 oz (50g) **glass noodles**

7 oz (200g) **firm tofu**

3½ oz (100g) **enoki mushrooms**, roughly chopped

½ **red onion**

2 tbsp **cornstarch**

2 tbsp **soy sauce**

1 tsp **sesame oil**

1 tbsp **Maggi seasoning**

10 tbsp **cold water**

½ cup finely chopped **fresh cilantro**, packed

½ **carrot**, finely grated

JIAOZI
(CLASSIC NORTHERN CHINESE DUMPLINGS)

SCAN FOR VIDEO

MAKES
32 jiaozi

PREP TIME
5 minutes

COOK TIME
60 minutes

To me, jiaozi are the quintessential baseline dumplings. You can make them with a gang of friends or all by yourself—and of course you can tweak the filling to your liking. No matter what, don't forget to make an extra batch because few foods freeze as well as jiaozi to make a fantastic instant meal!

DIRECTIONS

1. In a large bowl, whisk together the flour and salt. Add the water. (See note.) Mix together until the flour is fully hydrated. Cover with a damp towel and rest 30 minutes while making the filling.

2. On a lightly floured surface, knead the dough for 5 to 10 minutes. Cover and rest for 20 minutes.

3. Roll the dough into a long, thin log and divide into 32 pieces of equal size. (Scan QR code for video instruction.) On a lightly floured work surface, place each piece cut side down and flatten into a round disk with your palm. Repeat for all remaining dough pieces, keeping the surface lightly dusted.

4. With a small rolling pin, roll each piece into a thin, round dumpling skin about 3 inches (7.5cm) in diameter. Roll inward from the outside edge while rotating the skin. The goal is to thin out the edges and keep a thicker pillow in the center of the dumpling.

5. To the center of a dumpling wrapper, add 1 scant teaspoon of filling. Bring the edges of the wrapper together, surrounding the filling. Press the edges together to create 2 to 3 pleats on each side of the middle of the fold, working from the center to the corners of the dumpling. Transfer to a lightly dusted work surface, and cover loosely with plastic wrap. Repeat for all dumplings. Dumplings can be cooked immediately (boiled or steamed) or frozen for up to 6 weeks (see notes).

6. **To boil the dumplings,** fill a large pot about halfway with salted water and bring to a boil. Add the dumplings. Once the water comes back to a boil, add ½ cup cold water to "kill the boil." Repeat two more times. After killing the third boil, remove the dumplings from the water using a spider strainer or slotted spoon and transfer to a large serving plate. Do not stack dumplings to avoid sticking.

7. **To steam the dumplings,** line a bamboo or stainless steel steaming basket with a steamer liner or whole leaves of napa cabbage or lettuce. Fill with dumplings, leaving a little space between them. Place over a wok filled with about 1 cup boiling water over medium-high heat. Steam for 7 minutes. Remove the steamer from the heat and let sit, unopened, for 2 to 3 minutes. Work in batches if needed, making sure your water does not evaporate, and refill as needed.

2¾ cups **all-purpose flour**
(12.4 oz /350g)

1 tsp **salt** (0.2oz / 6g)

6½ fl oz (190g) **water**

1 batch **Jiaozi Filling** (page 71)
(For a veggie filling, make ½ batch **Tofu & Mushroom Lumpia Filling,** page 67)

3–5 large leaves of **napa cabbage** or **butter lettuce** (optional), for steaming

QUICK DIPPING SAUCE

¼ cup **dark Chinese vinegar**

2 tbsp **soy sauce**

1 tsp **toasted sesame oil**

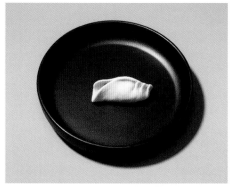

8. To make a quick dipping sauce, in a small bowl, combine all ingredients. Dumplings are also delicious served with Kuya Rafa's Sawsawan Dip (page 215), Ginger Scallion Crisp (page 223), and Chiu Chow Chili Oil (page 205).

NOTES: In step 1, add room temperature water for a chewy wrapper that is a bit harder to work with or boiling water for an easier folding process but a slightly pastier wrapper.

If you have sticking issues during folding, apply a little extra flour to the work surface.

Making a smaller quantity than this recipe is impractical, but you can scale this up as needed to make more.

Folded dumplings can be frozen in a single layer on a parchment-lined baking sheet. Once fully frozen, transfer to a zip-top bag and keep in the freezer for up to 2 months. Due to their small size, they defrost very quickly and can be cooked straight out of the freezer using the same method as fresh dumplings.

If your cooked dumplings stick together, try separating them in a bowl of water.

JIAOZI FILLING:
PORK & BOK CHOY

MAKES
Filling for 40–60 jiaozi

PREP TIME
10 minutes + 20 minutes inactive time

COOK TIME
None

DIRECTIONS

1. Place the bok choy in a large heatproof bowl and cover with boiling water. Let sit for 3 to 5 minutes. Drain and carefully squeeze out as much moisture as possible, taking care not to burn yourself. Return the bok choy to the bowl.

2. Add all remaining ingredients to the bowl. With two chopsticks or the back of a sturdy wooden spoon, mix the filling vigorously in the same direction for 5 minutes until it appears sticky and pasty.

3. Refrigerate for 20 minutes or up to overnight before making your dumplings.

7oz (200g) **bok choy**, finely chopped

½ lb (250g) **ground pork**

⅓ **leek**, white part only, finely chopped

1 tbsp **soy sauce**

2 tbsp **oyster sauce**

½ tbsp grated **fresh ginger**

2 tsp **cornstarch** or **all-purpose flour**

1 tsp **granulated sugar**

1 tsp **sesame oil**

½ tsp **white pepper**

¼ tsp **five spice powder**

¼ tsp **MSG**

¼ tsp **salt**

JIAOZI FILLING:
BEEF, CELERY & CARROT

MAKES
Filling for 40–60 jiaozi

PREP TIME
15 minutes + 20 minutes inactive time

COOK TIME
None

DIRECTIONS

1. In a large bowl, combine all ingredients. With two chopsticks or the back of a sturdy wooden spoon, mix the filling vigorously in the same direction for 5 minutes until it appears sticky and pasty

2. Refrigerate for 20 minutes or up to overnight before making your dumplings.

½ lb (250g) **ground beef**

1 **celery stalk**, finely chopped

⅓ **leek**, white part only, finely chopped

½ **carrot**, finely grated

1 tbsp **soy sauce**

1 tbsp grated **fresh ginger**

1 tbsp **oyster sauce**

2 tsp **cornstarch** or **all-purpose flour**

1 tsp **toasted sesame oil**

1 tsp **granulated sugar**

½ tsp **salt**

½ tsp **ground white pepper**

½ tsp **fennel seeds**

½ tsp **ground cumin**

¼ tsp **MSG**

SALTEÑAS
(BOLIVIAN HAND PIES)

SCAN FOR VIDEO

MAKES
12–16 salteñas

PREP TIME
40 minutes

COOK TIME
45 minutes

10 oz (300g) **chicken breast**

¼ cup **neutral cooking oil**

1 large **yellow onion,** diced

½ **yellow bell pepper,**
  finely diced

1 tbsp **sriracha**

1 tbsp **ground cumin**

1 tbsp **paprika**

1 tbsp **dried oregano**

1 large **potato,** diced

1 large **carrot** (optional), diced

Juice of 1 **lime**

½ tsp **salt** (or to taste)

½ tsp freshly cracked **black pepper** (20 cracks)

1 cup **frozen green peas**

½ cup chopped **fresh cilantro** (optional)

4 **hard-boiled eggs,** quartered lengthwise

½ cup **black olives,** sliced into rounds

FOR THE EGG WASH

1 **egg yolk**

1 tbsp **milk**

FOR THE DOUGH

2½ cups **all-purpose flour** (10.6oz / 300g)

1 tsp **paprika**

1 **egg**

1 tsp **salt**

¼ cup **granulated sugar** (2.1oz / 60g)

¼ cup melted **butter** (2.1oz / 60g)

½ cup **water** (4oz / 120g)

This dumpling hails straight from the Andes. The crust is reminiscent of a cracker and is often dyed golden with annatto seeds. The fillings and preparation methods can vary, but you will find versions of this chicken-and-veggie filling all over Bolivia. Salteñas are often bursting with juice (like a soup dumpling), but making that style is a bit more complex. This recipe keeps it simple and cuts the cooking time in half.

DIRECTIONS

1. Fill a large pot halfway with water and bring to a boil over high heat. Add the chicken breast and reduce heat to medium-low. Simmer for 15 minutes or until the chicken is fully cooked. Transfer the cooked chicken to a plate (discard the cooking liquid) and tent with foil. Let cool for 15 minutes. When cool enough to handle, shred the meat and set aside.

2. To the same pot over medium heat, add the oil, onion, bell pepper, sriracha, cumin, paprika, and oregano. Sauté for 2 to 3 minutes or until fragrant, then add the potato and carrot. Cook for 4 minutes, then add the lime juice, salt, pepper, and shredded chicken. Cook for 2 minutes, then remove from the heat. Stir in the green peas and cilantro, if using. Transfer the mixture to a bowl and set aside. (This is the filling for the salteñas.)

3. To make the dough, in a medium bowl, combine all ingredients. Mix until combined and the dough no longer sticks to your hands. Adjust the texture by adding more flour if needed. The dough should be firm yet pliable. Knead for 10 minutes by hand or 6 minutes in a stand mixer with the dough hook attached. Cover with a damp towel and rest for at least 15 minutes.

4. Divide the dough into 12 to 16 balls about the size of ping-pong balls. Roll out the balls into disks the size of your palm and ¹⁄₁₆ to ⅛ inch (1.5–2mm) thick. Keep the other dough balls covered with a damp towel while rolling out the disks. (Scan QR code for video instruction.)

5. To the center of each disk, add 1 tablespoon filling, 1 boiled egg quarter, and 4 to 5 olive slices.

6. Bring the edges of the dough together above the filling and pinch the dumpling shut along the seam. Create a generous edge about ½ inch (1.25cm) wide. To pleat the edge, fold one corner of the edge inward and pinch to secure the twist. Gently pinch again to create a new flap with the next section of unfolded dough, and fold inward. Repeat from the outer edges to the middle of the pinched dough. This creates a sealed dumpling with a beautiful pleated design.

7. Preheat the oven to 375°F (190°C). Line a baking sheet with parchment paper. Place the sealed salteñas on the prepared baking sheet. Brush lightly with egg wash. Bake for 15 to 20 minutes or until they are a deep golden brown on top.

8. Serve warm with Andean Green Salsa (page 74).

ANDEAN GREEN SALSA

MAKES
2 cups

PREP TIME
3 minutes

COOK TIME
None

When I enjoyed salteñas in Bolivia, they were often accompanied by fresh salsa made with an Andean herb called *inca muña*. While it can be hard to source overseas, a combo of common dried herbs and an optional pinch of nigella seeds gets pretty close!

DIRECTIONS

1. To a food processor, add the tomatoes, olive oil, shallot, garlic, mint, oregano, basil, salt, sugar, lime juice, and onion seeds (if using). Blend until the sauce is smooth and uniform in texture.

2. Transfer the mixture to a bowl, and stir in the jalapeño and cilantro. Salsa is ready to eat immediately, but tastes even better after resting in the fridge for 1 hour.

2 **green tomatoes,** quartered

1 tbsp **olive oil**

1 small **shallot,** quartered

1 clove **garlic**

½ tsp **dried mint**

½ tsp **dried oregano**

½ tsp **dried basil**

1 tsp **salt**

½ tsp **granulated sugar**

Juice of ½ **lime**

½ tsp **nigella onion seeds** (optional)

1 **jalapeño,** finely chopped

¼ cup finely chopped **fresh cilantro,** packed

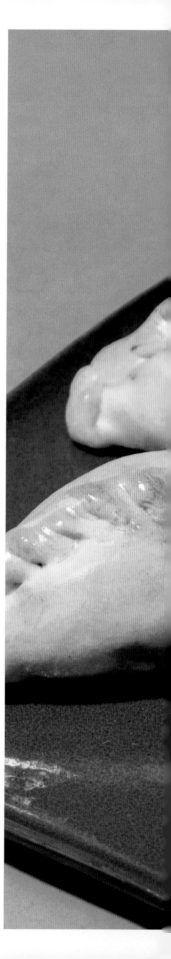

SHENG JIAN BAO
(STEAMED & FRIED LEAVENED DUMPLINGS)

SCAN FOR VIDEO

MAKES
32 bao

PREP TIME
40 minutes + 1 hour inactive time

COOK TIME
20 minutes

Some prefer fried dumplings; some prefer them steamed. But did you know you can have both? *Sheng jian bao,* literally translated as "raw fried dumplings," use a genius technique that is not only fast but also incredibly delicious, giving your bao wrappers a crispy bottom and fluffy top.

DIRECTIONS

1. Measure the flour into a large bowl. Scoop out ½ tablespoon flour, place in a small bowl, and set aside.

2. To the large bowl of flour, add the salt, sugar, and yeast, and whisk to combine. Add 7 ounces water. Mix until the flour is fully hydrated. Cover with a damp towel and rest for 20 minutes while you prepare the filling of your choice.

3. Knead the dough for 5 to 10 minutes, cover, and rest for 40 minutes more.

4. Turn the dough out onto a lightly floured work surface. Punch down the dough; roll it into a long, thin log; and divide into 32 equal pieces. (Scan QR code for video instruction.) Place each piece cut side down and flatten into a round disk with your palm. Repeat for all remaining dough pieces, keeping the surface lightly dusted with flour.

5. With a small rolling pin, roll each piece into a thin, roughly palm-sized round dumpling skin. Roll inward from the outside edge while rotating the skin. The goal is to thin out the edges and keep a thicker pillow of dough in the center of the dumpling wrapper.

6. Place a scant of 1 teaspoon of filling in the center of a dumpling wrapper. Pleat by pulling the edges of the dumpling into the center while rotating. Transfer to a lightly dusted work surface and keep loosely covered with plastic wrap. Repeat for all dumplings.

7. To the small bowl of reserved flour, add the remaining ¼ cup water. Whisk until fully dissolved to make a slurry.

8. Heat a large nonstick skillet (with a lid) over medium-high heat. Add 1 to 2 tablespoons cooking oil, and place as many dumplings into the skillet as you can fit without them touching each other. (You may need to work in batches.) Panfry for 2 to 3 minutes, uncovered, until the bottoms of the dumplings are golden brown. Add the water-flour slurry into the pan, cover with a lid, reduce the heat to medium, and steam for 6 minutes. Remove the lid, reduce the heat to low, and let remaining moisture evaporate. Remove from the skillet and sprinkle with toasted sesame seeds and scallions. Repeat with the remaining dumplings.

3 cups **all-purpose flour** (12.7oz / 360g), divided

1 tsp **salt**

½ tbsp **granulated sugar**

1½ tsp **instant yeast** (0.2oz / 5g)

7 fl oz (210g) + ¼ cup **water,** divided

1 batch **Jiaozi Filling** (page 71) (For a veggie filling, make ½ batch **Tofu & Mushroom Lumpia Filling,** page 67)

2-4 tbsp **neutral cooking oil**

1 tbsp **toasted sesame seeds**

1 tbsp **black toasted sesame seeds**

1-2 **scallions,** finely chopped

NOTE: Serve with dark Chinese vinegar, soy sauce, and sesame oil to taste. Kuya Rafa's Sawsawan Dip (page 215), Ginger Scallion Crisp (page 223) and Chiu Chow Chili Oil (page 205) are also great with bao.

Embracing Community: the Joy of Dumpling Making

I have lost count of how many times I made dumplings by now. Triple digits for sure, though. Do I remember every time I've made a small batch for myself? Definitely not, even though that makes up the bulk of my dumpling-making experience. Do I remember every time I've made dumplings with friends? Every single time.

One of the first things I learned about making dumplings is that it's a team sport. The Chinese friends and families who first showed me the basics of making *jiaozi* emphasized how each person had a very clear task. First, one person makes the filling while another prepares the dough. When time comes to fold the dumplings, people almost intuitively arrange themselves into an assembly line.

There is a *divider,* who portions out the dough, rolls it into logs, and slices those into neat little balls that are pressed into a coin with one swift, confident motion. (Although the latter part was always a favorite to pass off to the occasional kid hanging around.) The coins of dough are then passed to the *roller,* who rolls them into disks with thick centers and thin edges, a shape essential for a well-balanced dumpling wrapper. I have seen countless people do this with surgical precision while surrounded by a light cloud of flour dust.

The finished wrappers are finally passed on to a group of *folders,* who gather cheerfully around a giant bowl of filling and blanket tray after tray in freshly made dumplings. On particularly busy days, a second or even third *roller* is required.

Finally, there is always the big moment when the completed dumplings are dropped in a giant pot of bubbling water. What follows is the almost sacred ritual of "the three boils," where cool water is added just as the water starts boiling three times before the dumplings are removed. This achieves the perfect texture and doneness without overcooking the dumplings. It's one of those old-school Chinese home cooking wisdoms that just works, like measuring rice water with your finger.

The dumplings you make with friends are not always pretty. In fact, there is always that one friend who is truly terrible at folding them (to everyone's amusement). It's all part of the charm of collective dumpling making—I like to think of the ugly dumplings as the lucky ones. But the times you have making dumplings with your friends are always the best ones.

There are also the occasional few who like to make dumplings on their own. A friend of mine lived with a Chinese host family once. His host dad would sit down in front of the TV and just make dumplings for an hour—every single night. Needless to say, the freezer was always stocked.

I, too, understand the draw of making dumplings by yourself. In those cases, what can be a beautiful mess surrounded by friends turns into a meticulous labor of love. Every single flick of your wrist a routine, every fold perfectly rehearsed and precisely placed. There is something zen about it; you might even enter the magical flow state my favorite productivity gurus like to talk about.

Always remember that a dumpling in its basic form is an empty canvas for you to express your current culinary mood. You want something spicy and rich? Stuff it with decadent fatty meat, wrap in a hearty layer, panfry until crispy, and cover in chili crisp. Want something light? Go for a veggie filling, a paper-thin wonton wrapper, and dip in vinegar after gently steaming. The world of dumplings truly has it all.

No matter what you are looking for on your cooking journey—whether it's community, tranquility, nourishment, or all of the above—dumplings are one of the most direct forms of experiencing all the wonderful human things food can be, and they taste damn delicious, too.

OVEN-BAKED SAMOSAS

SCAN FOR VIDEO

MAKES

12 samosas

PREP TIME

45 minutes + 15 minutes to rest dough

COOK TIME

25 minutes

How to scratch that samosa itch without turning your place into a deep-frying inferno? That's right, with this baked samosa recipe! Whether you choose to fill your samosas with meat or a more traditional potato-based filling, this low-stress recipe is just what your next picnic might need.

1 cup + 2 tbsp **all-purpose flour** (6.2oz / 175g)

1 tbsp **neutral cooking oil**

¼ tsp **salt**

3¼ oz (90g) **hot water**

1 **egg yolk**

½ tsp **milk** or **water**

1 batch **Samosa Filling** (page 82)

1 tbsp **nigella** or **sesame seeds** (optional)

DIRECTIONS

1. In a large bowl, combine the flour, oil, and salt. Whisk to combine, then rub between your fingers until no large clumps of oil remain.

2. Bring the hot water to a boil and add it to the flour mixture right away. Bring the mixture together with a wooden spoon or spatula. (Be careful not to burn yourself.) Once the dough is cool enough to safely handle, knead for 1 minute until no dry flour remains, and shape into a ball. The dough should be quite stiff but still pliable. Place in an airtight container and rest for at least 15 minutes.

3. Meanwhile, in a small bowl, combine the egg yolk and milk. Preheat the oven to 375°F (190°C) and line a baking sheet with parchment paper.

4. Divide the dough into 6 equal balls, each about 1½ ounces (40g) in weight. Working with one ball at a time, roll out each one into a thin disk about 7 inches (17cm) in diameter and ¹⁄₁₆ inch (1.5mm) thick. Cut the disk in half, creating two half circles. (Scan QR code for video instruction.) Place one of the half circles on a lightly dusted working surface. Place 1 level tablespoon of filling in the center of the dough.

5. Fold both pointy ends over the filling, forming an open cone shape. Seal the cone by pressing together the dough around the open end tightly. Try to not trap any air inside. Once sealed, turn the samosa seam side down. Cover the finished samosas with a damp kitchen towel. Continue for the remaining dough.

6. With a pastry brush, apply a thin film of egg yolk to all samosas. With the tip of a knife, gently score the top of each samosa to create a small ¼-inch (5mm) steam vent. Sprinkle with a small pinch of nigella seeds.

7. Place the samosas on the prepared baking sheet, and bake for 20 to 25 minutes or until golden brown on top. Rest for 10 minutes before eating.

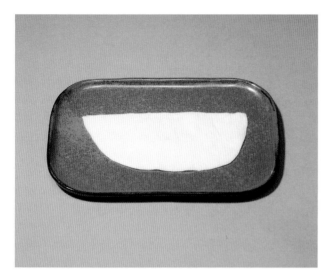

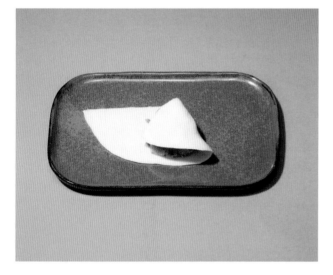

SAMOSA FILLING:
UZBEK-STYLE BEEF

MAKES
Filling for 12 samosas

PREP TIME
10 minutes

COOK TIME
None

DIRECTIONS

1. Mince the meat by chopping into very fine chunks, about ⅛ x ⅛ inch (3 x 3mm).

2. In a large bowl, combine the meat, onion, cumin, chili flakes, salt, MSG, and cornstarch. Knead vigorously for 3 minutes or until well combined.

NOTE: You can substitute ground beef for this recipe and omit step 1. However, it is highly recommended you try mincing meat by hand; the result is far superior.

6oz (175g) lean **beef** (see note)

1 small **onion,** finely diced

½ tsp **ground cumin**

½ tsp **red chili flakes**

¼ tsp **salt**

⅛ tsp **MSG**

½ tbsp **cornstarch**

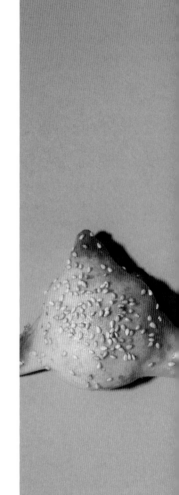

SAMOSA FILLING:
POTATO MASALA

MAKES
Filling for 12 samosas

PREP TIME
10 minutes

COOK TIME
20 minutes

DIRECTIONS

1. Place the potatoes in a large pot and cover with salted water. Bring to a boil, then cook over medium-high heat for 15 minutes or until fork-tender. Drain and let cool for 15 minutes.

2. Meanwhile, in a small saucepan, heat the clarified butter, curry powder, cumin, and garam masala over medium-high heat for 2 minutes or until the butter has fully melted and the spice mix has begun to sizzle and smell fragrant.

3. In a large bowl, roughly mash the potatoes with the spiced butter, salt, and MSG until no large lumps remain. Add the peas, spinach, cilantro, green chili, and lime juice. Mix to combine.

½ lb (250g) **potatoes,** peeled and quartered

1 tbsp **clarified butter**

1 tsp **curry powder**

¼ tsp **ground cumin**

¼ tsp **garam masala**

½ tsp **salt**

¼ tsp **MSG**

¼ cup **frozen peas**

1 cup **frozen chopped spinach**

¼ cup finely chopped **fresh cilantro,** packed

1 **green chili,** finely chopped

½ tbsp **lime juice**

PORK & SHRIMP WONTONS
WITH CHILI OIL

SCAN FOR VIDEO

MAKES
40-50 wontons

PREP TIME
10 minutes

COOK TIME
15 minutes

I once had a truly legendary bowl of wonton noodle soup in Hong Kong. The bad news? It would be nearly impossible to re-create. The good news? That only goes for the super-complex broth. These classic surf-and-turf wontons can easily be made at home. And fortunately, smothering them in chili oil might make them even more of a crowd pleaser.

DIRECTIONS

1. To a food processor, add the pork, oyster sauce, soy sauce, ginger, light green parts of the scallions, sesame oil, and white pepper. Blend until a homogenous but not completely smooth paste forms.

2. Transfer the filling mixture to a medium bowl and fold in the chopped shrimp

3. Place 1 teaspoon of filling in the center of a single wonton wrapper. Wet two adjacent edges of the wrapper with water. Fold the wonton in half diagonally, trying to squeeze out as much air as possible. Wet the two sharp corners and bring them together. Press to seal firmly. Set the wonton aside and cover with a damp kitchen towel until ready to cook. Repeat until you run out of wonton wrappers. (Scan QR code for video instruction.)

4. Fill a large pot or wok two-thirds full with water and bring to a simmer over medium-high heat. Working in batches, gently drop in the dumplings and simmer for 3 minutes after the water has come back up to a soft boil. Drain and divide evenly among 2 to 4 serving bowls.

5. Serve topped with chili oil, soy sauce, scallion greens, and cilantro (if using).

9 oz (250g) **ground pork**

1 tbsp **oyster sauce**

1 tbsp **soy sauce**

1-inch (2cm) piece **fresh ginger**, minced

2 **scallions**, finely chopped, light and dark green parts divided

1 tsp **sesame oil**

½ tsp **ground white pepper**

3½ oz (100g) raw **shrimp** (any size), peeled and deveined, chopped

1 package **wonton wrappers**, thawed (about 40-50 sheets)

TO SERVE

3-4 tbsp **Chiu Chow Chili Oil** (page 205) or **Chili Crisp** (page 204)

3-4 tbsp **soy sauce**

¼ cup chopped **fresh cilantro** (optional)

NOTE: For a more advanced wonton folding technique, scan here.

SCAN FOR VIDEO

MOMDONG'S
RUSSIAN PIROZHKI

SCAN FOR VIDEO

MAKES
16 pirozhki

PREP TIME
40 minutes + 45 minutes
    inactive time

COOK TIME
25 minutes

These delicious Eastern European hand pies are so ubiquitous that (at least back in Soviet times) you'd be hard-pressed to find a train station without a few babushkas selling fried or baked *pirozhki* to hungry travelers. The fillings are often savory— meat, or veggies and eggs—but they can be sweet as well. I might be a little biased here, but I'm convinced my mom makes the very best ones, so this recipe was developed with her help and approval.

DIRECTIONS

1. In a large bowl, whisk the flour and salt. Add the butter and incorporate by rubbing flour and butter between your hands until the mixture resembles wet sand.

2. In a medium bowl, combine the milk, egg, yeast, and sugar. Mix the milk mixture with the flour mixture and knead for about 5 minutes until you get a rough but homogenous dough. Cover and rest for 15 minutes on the counter.

3. Knead for another 5 minutes in the bowl. Cover and refrigerate for at least 30 minutes but no longer than 4 hours. Meanwhile, prepare the filling and line a baking sheet with parchment paper.

4. After removing the dough from the refrigerator, punch it down and knead it inside the bowl for 1 to 2 minutes. Turn the dough out onto a lightly floured surface. Roll the dough into a log and divide it into 16 equal pieces, each about 1½ ounces (40g) in weight. Shape each piece into a ball.

5. On a lightly floured work surface, roll out each ball into a disk about ⅛ inch (2mm) thick and 4 to 5 inches (10–12cm) in diameter. (Scan QR code for video instruction.) Place one heaping tablespoon of filling in the center of the disk. Bring together the top and bottom edges of the disk over the filling and pleat or pinch shut.

6. Turn the pirozhok seam side down and gently pat it into a plump shape with your hands. Transfer to the prepared baking sheet. Keep the filled pirozhki covered with a damp kitchen towel as you prepare the remaining pirozhki. (You may need to use two baking sheets.)

7. Preheat the oven to 350°F (180°C). To make the egg wash, in a small bowl, lightly beat the egg yolk and the milk. Apply a thin layer of egg wash to all pirozhki. Bake for 20 to 25 minutes or until golden brown.

3 cups **all-purpose flour**
 (12.7oz / 360g)

1 tsp **salt**

1 stick **butter** (4oz / 115g),
 at room temperature

½ cup **milk** (4.2oz / 120g),
 at room temperature

1 large **egg**

1 packet **instant yeast**
 (0.25oz / 7g)

2 tbsp **granulated sugar**

1 batch **Pirozhki Filling**
 (page 89)

FOR THE EGG WASH
1 **egg yolk**

1 tbsp **milk**

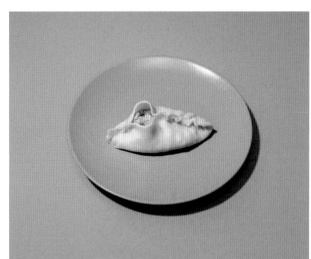

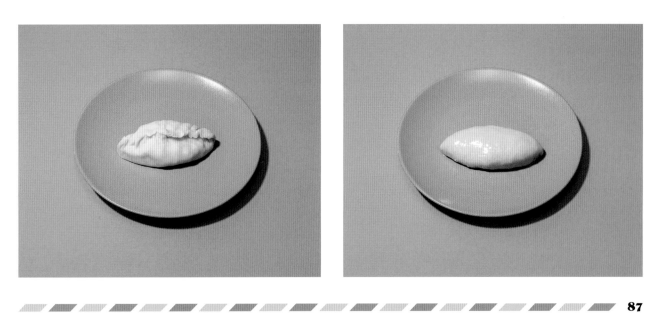

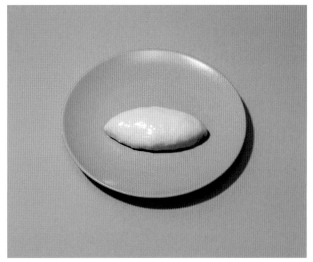

PIROZHKI FILLING:
CHICKEN

MAKES
Filling for 16 pirozhki

PREP TIME
30 minutes

COOK TIME
35 minutes

DIRECTIONS

1. Line a baking sheet with parchment paper. Preheat the oven to 375°F (190°C).

2. Sprinkle the chicken legs with salt on all sides. Arrange on the prepared baking sheet, skin side up. Add the halved onions to the baking sheet, cut side down. Bake for 35 minutes or until the chicken skin is golden brown and crisp.

3. Meanwhile, prepare the rice according to package instructions. Set aside.

4. Remove the chicken from the oven and let cool for 20 minutes. When cool enough to handle, remove the meat from the bones and roughly shred it. (Discard the skin and bones or keep for stock.)

5. Chop the shredded chicken and roasted onions into fine pieces. Transfer to a large bowl and add the cooked rice, dill, and pepper. Using a sturdy tool like a wooden spoon, mix vigorously to combine into a semipaste-like consistency. Taste and season with more salt if needed. Refrigerate until ready to use.

3 bone-in, skin-on **chicken legs** (thigh and drumstick)

1 tsp **salt**, plus more to taste

3 **red onions**, peeled and halved

½ cup **white rice**

½ cup chopped **fresh dill**, tender stems and leaves only, packed

1½ tsp freshly cracked **black pepper** (30 cracks)

PIROZHKI FILLING:
CABBAGE & EGG

MAKES
Filling for 16 pirozhki

PREP TIME
10 minutes

COOK TIME
20 minutes

DIRECTIONS

1. Place the eggs in a saucepan and add water to cover. Bring to a boil over high heat. Boil the eggs for 8 minutes. Transfer to an ice water bath for 5 minutes and peel. In a medium bowl, mash the eggs with a fork. Set aside.

2. Place the cabbage in a large bowl and sprinkle with the salt. Mix and knead with your hands for 5 minutes until the cabbage has softened.

3. In a large saucepan, melt the butter and add the softened cabbage. Sauté the cabbage, stirring occasionally, for 10 minutes or until it just begins to caramelize.

4. Return the cabbage to the bowl. Add the mashed eggs and mix to incorporate. Taste and add salt, if needed. Refrigerate until ready to use.

3 large **eggs**

1½ lb (700g) finely shredded **green cabbage**

1 tsp **salt**, plus more to taste

2 tbsp **butter** (0.9oz / 25g)

Street Food

Nothing beats grabbing a delicious, affordable snack while exploring a new place somewhere in the world. No wonder street food has evolved from a descriptive term to a whole art form in itself. There are literally countless iconic dishes around the globe that would fit in this category in one way or another. This chapter offers my take on a select few of those on-the-go meals that are especially near and dear to me.

Berlin-Style Chicken Döner Kebab **95**
    Döner Sauce **96**
    Döner Bread **97**

Karelian Kalitki **99**
    Salmon Filling **100**
    Potato Filling **101**

Pretzels **103**

Scallion Pancakes **104**

Anti-Perfectionist Pad Thai **111**

Flammkuchen **113**

Cuban Sandwich, Germanized **115**

Forbidden Chow Mein **117**

Street Food: the Crown Jewel of Food Travel

If you want to truly get to know the soul of a place's food culture, you don't go for the fancy, award-winning restaurants (as good as they might be)—you take to the streets. Not every place is blessed with the climate or infrastructure needed to be an around-the-year street food paradise, but every place will have its signature grab-and-go meals!

THE FLAVOR OF MY CHILDHOOD

Berlin-style döner kebab has earned a very special place in my heart and this book. You can read more about it in my little essay on this street food sandwich that undoubtedly defined my culinary upbringing (page 108).

Coming up with a recipe was not an easy task—as a Berliner, I have my own very high standards to meet. But if you are down with trying chicken kebab (one of the two main styles in Berlin, with the OG being veal), I believe I have just the right recipe for you.

What really sells it is the sauce. If you grew up eating döner in Berlin, I promise it will instantly bring up memories (maybe involving late nights out). Of course, döner would also not be döner without the signature quarter-circle bread. (Don't worry, I have a recipe for that, too.)

GERMAN STREET FOOD

Is döner all Germans eat on the go? It certainly isn't. The default snack is a simple cold sandwich, which is nothing unusual. But while most of the world prefers sliced bread for convenience, Germans are a bit more serious about their bread. Among the many choices, one reigns supreme in terms of cultural importance: the **pretzel.** Try my recipe and devour a fresh home-baked pretzel with butter and chives—one of life's great simple pleasures.

If you ever make it to a city fair or Christmas market in Germany, a seductive smoky, savory smell will likely immediately lure you in. If you are wondering where it comes from—it's **flammkuchen.** This topped flatbread is a specialty from the Alsace, the border region of Germany and France. Superficially speaking, it's Germany and France's answer to pizza, except the sauce is a sour cream base, and it's topped with bacon bits and heaps of onions. The dough is not yeasted and almost resembles a cracker more than a bread, making this dish both light and crispy yet rich and hearty.

Another recipe you will find in this section is my eclectic **Cuban sandwich** made using typically German ingredients. When I first tried a Cuban sandwich, it was love at first bite, and to my delight, all elements were found in German cooking. It serves more as an encouragement for you to never be afraid to play around with local ingredients in the kitchen, even if it might seem like an odd choice at first.

GOING GLOBAL

Globally speaking, I have always been most drawn to the street food cultures of Asia. Coming in all flavors, shapes, and colors, they just hit the spot for me.

One of my favorites would absolutely be the flaky **scallion pancake.** I would often grab one on my way to class as a student in Beijing, and I've always thought of it as China's savory answer to the croissant.

On a busy day, I would often sit down in a hole-in-the-wall spot next to my university and chow down on a quick bowl of **chow mein**—a dish I loved way before I ever even considered moving to China. In this chapter, I share a controversial interpretation of chow mein using Italian pasta—which you may be shocked to find works surprisingly well!

Speaking of Asian noodle dishes, **pad thai** has got to be one of the first options that comes to mind for most. If you are willing to sacrifice some authenticity, you can make a very decent version of it in about half an hour. But the true reason I've included it in this book is its story. Did you know pad thai was created less than a century ago by a Thai nationalist dictator as a new national dish? And, clearly, it actually worked? I am a sucker for a good food-origin story, and this is one of the best.

Finally, I leave you with my mom's recipe for **kalitki,** or Karelian pasties. Karelia is a region stretching from modern-day Finland into Russia. It originally had its own distinct culture which has, for the most part, diluted into Russian or Finnish society around it. One of its legacies, though, remains: the humble but visually pleasing Karelian pasty, a popular regional convenience food.

BERLIN-STYLE
CHICKEN DÖNER KEBAB

SERVES
4

PREP TIME
30 minutes

COOK TIME
45 minutes

This is a recipe for the taste of my childhood. Or at least as close as you can come to it in a regular kitchen. Chicken (instead of veal) is what makes this recipe more accessible for home cooks, and with the right bread and assortment of veggies, it will invoke some serious nostalgia in Berliners. But the sauce is what really brings it home—I highly recommend using it on other sandwiches or as a dip or dressing!

DIRECTIONS

1. Preheat the oven to 375°F (190°C). Line a baking sheet with parchment paper.

2. In a large bowl, toss the chicken drumsticks with the mayonnaise, paprika, chili flakes, garlic powder, dried herbs, ½ teaspoon salt, and 1 teaspoon sugar until evenly coated. Arrange the chicken on the prepared baking sheet, spacing the drumsticks out evenly.

3. In the same large bowl, toss the carrot, eggplant, and potato with the olive oil, soy sauce, and remaining ½ teaspoon salt and 1½ teaspoon sugar. Add the vegetables to the baking sheet, arranging them around and in between the chicken.

4. Roast for 30 minutes, flipping the chicken halfway through cooking. Remove the baking sheet from the oven and rest for 5 minutes.

5. Hold each drumstick pointy side up, and using a knife, gently slice the meat from the bones. Discard the bones (or keep for stock) and roughly chop the meat into bite-sized chunks.

6. In a large bowl, combine the meat with the roasted veggies and the drippings from the baking sheet. Mix well and return to the baking sheet. Roast for 10 minutes more or until slightly crispy.

7. Meanwhile, slice the döner bread quarters horizontally, stopping just short of the edge so that the top and bottom halves remain connected (like a hot dog bun). Toast the exterior of each döner bread in a sandwich press or in a frying pan while pressing the bread down with a second pan.

8. To assemble, open each piece of bread, and spread about 1 tablespoon of sauce on one half. Briefly close and open the bread to spread sauce on both sides.

9. Add 2 to 3 heaping tablespoons of the roasted chicken and vegetable mix, followed by red onion, lettuce, parsley, red cabbage, tomatoes, and cucumber, to taste. Sprinkle with a pinch of salt and drizzle with more sauce, if desired.

4 **chicken drumsticks**
(1.3lb / 600g in total)

¼ cup **mayonnaise**
(2.1oz / 60g)

1 tsp **smoked paprika**

1 tsp **red chili flakes**

½ tsp **garlic powder**

½ tsp **dried marjoram**

½ tsp **dried rosemary**

½ tsp **dried thyme**

1 tsp **dried basil**

1 tsp **salt**, divided

2½ tsp **granulated sugar**, divided

1 small **carrot**, finely diced

1 small **eggplant**, finely diced

1 large **potato**, finely diced

3 tbsp **olive oil**, divided

2 tbsp **soy sauce**

TO SERVE

1 round **Döner Bread** (page 96) or large, fluffy flatbread, cut into quarters

Döner Sauce (page 97) or **ranch dressing**, to taste

½ **red onion**, thinly sliced

½ head of **iceberg lettuce**, shredded

¼ cup finely chopped **fresh parsley**, packed

¼ small head of **red cabbage**, shredded

2 medium **tomatoes**, diced

½ **cucumber**, julienned

DÖNER SAUCE

MAKES
1½ cups

PREP TIME
5 minutes

COOK TIME
None

1 cup **mayonnaise**
(8oz / 225g)

½ cup **plain yogurt**
(4oz / 115g)

¼ tsp **salt**

¼ tsp **MSG**

½ tbsp **agave syrup** (or corn
syrup or granulated sugar)

1 tsp **dried dill**

1 tsp **dried mint**

1 tsp **dried oregano**

¼ tsp **garlic powder**

1 tsp **onion powder**

DIRECTIONS

1. In a medium bowl, combine all ingredients and mix well.

2. Transfer to an airtight container and refrigerate for at least 1 hour or, even better, overnight. Sauce can be stored in the fridge for at least 3 days.

DÖNER BREAD

MAKES
2 flatbreads (8 servings)

PREP TIME
15 minutes + 90 minutes
inactive time

COOK TIME
20 minutes

3½ cups **all-purpose flour**
(16.8oz / 475g)

1 packet **instant yeast**
(0.25oz / 7g)

1 tsp **salt** (0.25oz / 7g)

1 tbsp **sugar** (0.5oz / 15g)

1¼ cups + 2 tbsp **milk**
(11.3oz / 320g), room
temperature, divided

1 tbsp **olive oil**

3-4 tbsp **corn flour**

½ tsp **sesame seeds**

¼ tsp **nigella seeds**

DIRECTIONS

1. Line 2 baking sheets with parchment paper. In the bowl of a stand mixer, combine the flour, yeast, salt, and sugar. Hand whisk to combine.

2. Add 1¼ cups milk and knead with a dough hook attachment for 2 minutes on low. Add the olive oil and knead for another 8 minutes on medium-high.

3. Divide the resulting dough in half. Roll each half into a ball. Cover with a damp kitchen towel and proof for 30 minutes. Punch down the dough and roll each ball out into a thick disk with a diameter of about 10 inches (25cm). With damp hands, lightly moisten the surface of each disk, and sprinkle with corn flour. Place the disks on the prepared baking sheets, corn-flour side down. Cover with damp kitchen towels and proof for 60 minutes or until the dough has almost doubled in size.

4. Preheat the oven to 450°F (230°C). Gently brush the disks with the remaining 2 tablespoons milk and sprinkle with sesame and nigella seeds.

5. Bake one at a time for 10 minutes each or until golden brown. Let cool for at least 30 minutes before slicing. Cut each flatbread into quarters to get the classic triangular Berlin-style döner shape (or eat as desired).

KARELIAN KALITKI

SCAN FOR VIDEO

MAKES
14 kalitki

PREP TIME
30 minutes + 20 minutes
inactive time

COOK TIME
25 minutes

Somewhere between an open-faced sandwich and a dumpling, kalitki are very hard to fit into a category. What I can promise is that this convenient comfort food packs a lot of classic Nordic ingredients into a delightful bite-sized hand pie, and it's sure to spark your guests' interest with its striking appearance.

1 cup **rye flour** (5oz / 140g)

¾ cup **all-purpose flour**
(3oz / 85g)

¼ tsp **salt**

½ cup **buttermilk**
(4.2oz / 120g)

¼ cup **water** (2.1oz / 60g)

1 batch **Kalitki Filling**, either
salmon (page 100) or potato
(page 101)

3 tbsp **sour cream**

1 large **egg**

2 tbsp melted **butter**

Chopped **fresh dill** or **chives**,
to taste

DIRECTIONS

1. In a large bowl, combine the rye flour, all-purpose flour, salt, buttermilk, and water. Knead for 3 to 5 minutes until a shaggy dough forms. Cover with a damp kitchen towel, and rest while you prepare your filling (or for at least 20 minutes).

2. Meanwhile, preheat the oven to 375°F (190°C) and line a baking sheet with parchment paper.

3. On a lightly floured surface, briefly knead the dough and divide into 14 equal pieces. Roll each piece into a thin oval, about 5 inches (12.5cm) long and 4 inches (10cm wide). (Scan QR code for video instruction.)

4. To the center of each disk of dough, add 1 to 2 tablespoons of filling. Pinch one of the sides to form a pointy end. Create about 8 folds along the top half of the circle, ending with a second pointy end. Do the same on the bottom half so that the filling is still visible but surrounded by pleated dough. Place the filled kalitki on the prepared baking sheet. Repeat for all pieces of dough.

5. In a small bowl, whisk together the sour cream and egg. Brush the egg wash over the open-faced filling of the kalitki. Bake for 20 to 25 minutes or until the edges are golden brown.

6. Immediately after removing the kalitki from the oven, brush each one with melted butter and sprinkle with fresh dill or chives. Cover with a kitchen towel and let the kalitki cool and soften for at least 15 minutes before eating.

KALITKI FILLING:
SALMON

MAKES
Filling for 14 kalitki

PREP TIME
5 minutes

COOK TIME
3 minutes

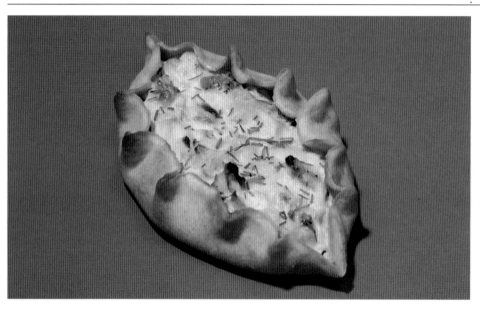

7oz (200g) skinless
  hot-smoked salmon

1 large **egg**

½ cup **sour cream**
  (about 24% fat)

⅓ **leek,** light green part only,
  finely chopped

DIRECTIONS

1. In a medium bowl, combine all ingredients. Mash with a fork until homogenous.
   Refrigerate until ready to use.

KALITKI FILLING:
POTATO

MAKES
Filling for 14 kalitki

PREP TIME
5 minutes

COOK TIME
30 minutes

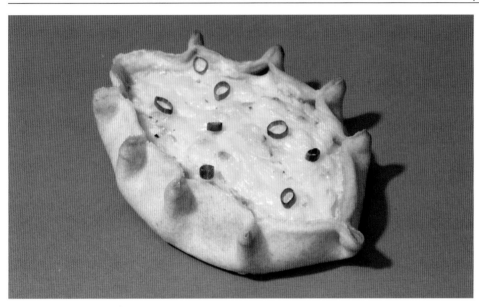

4 medium starchy **potatoes** (unpeeled)

1 **egg**

½ cup **sour cream** (about 24% fat)

1 tbsp softened **butter**

1 **leek,** white part only, finely chopped

1 tsp **salt**

1 tsp freshly cracked **black pepper** (20 cracks)

DIRECTIONS

1. Place the potatoes in a large pot, and add water to cover by at least 2 inches (5cm). Bring to a boil over high heat, then reduce heat to maintain a low boil. Cook the potatoes for 25 minutes or until fork-tender, and drain.

2. Once potatoes are just cool enough to handle, remove the skins. In a large bowl, mash the potatoes together with the egg, sour cream, butter, chopped leek, salt, and pepper until homogenous. Refrigerate until ready to use.

PRETZELS

MAKES
6 pretzels

PREP TIME
30 minutes + 80 minutes inactive time

COOK TIME
20 minutes

There are many foods that cause me to wonder who first came up with the idea to make them. Pretzels are on top of that list. Why would anyone want to dip unbaked bread into what is essentially drain cleaner? Of course, the reason is that it somehow makes the bread even more delicious—but you wouldn't know that unless you tried it! Whatever the origin story, the use of lye gives soft pretzels their signature shiny finish and unmistakable flavor.

DIRECTIONS

1. In the bowl of a stand mixer fitted with a dough hook, combine the flour, yeast, salt, sugar, butter, and milk. Knead for 2 minutes on medium-low speed, and then increase the speed to high and knead for 8 minutes.

2. Cover the bowl of your stand mixer with plastic wrap and place it in the oven with just the light on to proof for 30 minutes. Meanwhile, line a baking sheet with parchment paper.

3. With damp hands, divide the dough in 6 equal pieces and roll into balls. To form the pretzels, roll each ball into a "snake." Roll back and forth starting from the center, increasing pressure as you reach the ends until you have a long, tapered torpedo shape about 20 inches (50cm) long. Repeat this process if needed. Take the two ends, bring them together, and gently cross over each other. Twist ends once, gently bring them down to the front and attach the two arms to the base line by pressing firmly.

4. Place pretzels on the prepared baking sheet. Proof uncovered for 20 minutes on the counter, and then transfer to the refrigerator to proof for an additional 30 minutes.

5. *When preparing the alkaline solution, wear food-safe gloves and safety glasses.* To prepare the alkaline solution, in a medium bowl, carefully combine the lye and cold water. Dunk each pretzel in the solution for 5 seconds on each side, allow the excess liquid to drip off, and transfer to a lightly greased cooling rack.

6. Optional: for a traditional presentation style, score the thickest part of each pretzel. The cut should be about ½ inch (1.25cm) deep and 3 to 4 inches (6cm) in length, following the curvature of the pretzel. Lightly sprinkle the thickest parts of the pretzel with coarse salt.

7. Place the baking sheet in a cold oven. Set the oven to 355°F (180°C) and bake for 20 minutes (from the time you place the baking sheet in the cold oven) or until deeply brown on the outside. Serve with butter and chives for a minimalist-but-classic experience, or dip in Obazda (page 213).

2½ cups **all-purpose flour** (12.34oz / 350g)

1 packet **instant yeast** (0.25oz / 7g)

¾ tsp **salt** (0.2oz / 5.5g)

½ tbsp **granulated sugar**

1 oz (30g) softened **butter**

¾ cup + 1 tbsp **milk** (7oz / 200g), at room temperature

1 tbsp **coarse salt**

Butter (optional), to serve

Chopped **fresh chives** (optional), to serve

FOR THE ALKALINE SOLUTION

3.5 oz (100g) **food-grade lye** (36% sodium hydroxide solution)

3¾ cups (900ml) cold **water**

SAFETY NOTE: Lye is highly caustic and should be handled with care. Wear food-safe gloves and protective eyewear when working with lye. Work in a well-ventilated area, and use equipment made from nonreactive materials (stainless steel, heavy-duty plastic, or glass; no aluminum).

SCALLION PANCAKES

SCAN FOR VIDEO

MAKES
4 pancakes

PREP TIME
40 minutes + 40 minutes
inactive time

COOK TIME
25 minutes

Flaky pastries will make many think of croissants or danishes. But my favorite from this category is undoubtedly the Chinese scallion pancake. Not only is the method a lot simpler than the labor of love that a homemade croissant would be, but the reward is delightful, flaky, scallion-infused goodness. Pro tip: par-fry and freeze your scallion pancakes for almost instant breakfast happiness!

2½ cups **all-purpose flour** (10.9oz / 300g)

1 tsp **salt**

1 cup boiling **water**

3 **scallions**, finely minced

¼ cup **neutral cooking oil**

FOR THE ROUX

3 tbsp **neutral cooking oil** or lard

2 tbsp **all-purpose flour**

½ tsp **salt**

½ tsp **five spice powder**

DIRECTIONS

1. In a medium bowl, combine the flour, salt, and boiling water. With a wooden spoon, mix until combined. Taking care not to burn yourself, knead the dough for 5 to 10 minutes. Roll into a ball, cover with a damp towel, and rest for 30 minutes.

2. Meanwhile, make the roux. In a small saucepan over medium-low heat, combine the oil, flour, salt, and five spice powder. Whisk until combined. Cook for 3 minutes until large bubbles appear, remove from heat, and set aside.

3. Turn the dough out onto a lightly floured work surface. Briefly knead the dough, and then divide it into 4 equal portions. (Scan QR code for video instruction.) Roll into balls and rest, covered with a damp towel, for 5 to 10 minutes.

4. Working one at a time, roll each ball into an elongated oval. Try to get the dough as thin as possible without tearing. Orient the dough so that the longer side is perpendicular to you.

5. Brush a thin layer of roux over the dough. Sprinkle a thin layer of scallions, leaving about ½ inch (1.25cm) of dough exposed on the edge that is furthest away from you. Carefully and tightly roll the dough, starting at the long edge closest to your body and rolling away from you. You will have a long, scallion-filled tube. Coil the tube like a snail, and tuck the end of the tube underneath the rolled-up dough. With a rolling pin, press down to shape the coiled dough into a puck. Flatten and gently roll out the dough one more time until the scallions are visible through the dough but do not pierce the dough. The diameter of your final pancake should be 7 to 10 inches (18–25cm). Repeat for the remaining 3 pancakes.

6. You can now stack your pancakes, separated by layers of parchment paper, and freeze them in a zip-top bag for later use—or proceed straight to the next step.

7. In a 10-inch (20cm) skillet over medium heat, heat enough oil for a shallow fry and add a pancake. Pressing the pancake down occasionally, fry on the first side for 3 to 5 minutes or until lightly golden on the bottom. Flip and repeat on the opposite side. Fry for another 1 to 2 minutes on both sides. Once cooked, remove, rest for 3 minutes, slice like a pizza, and serve hot.

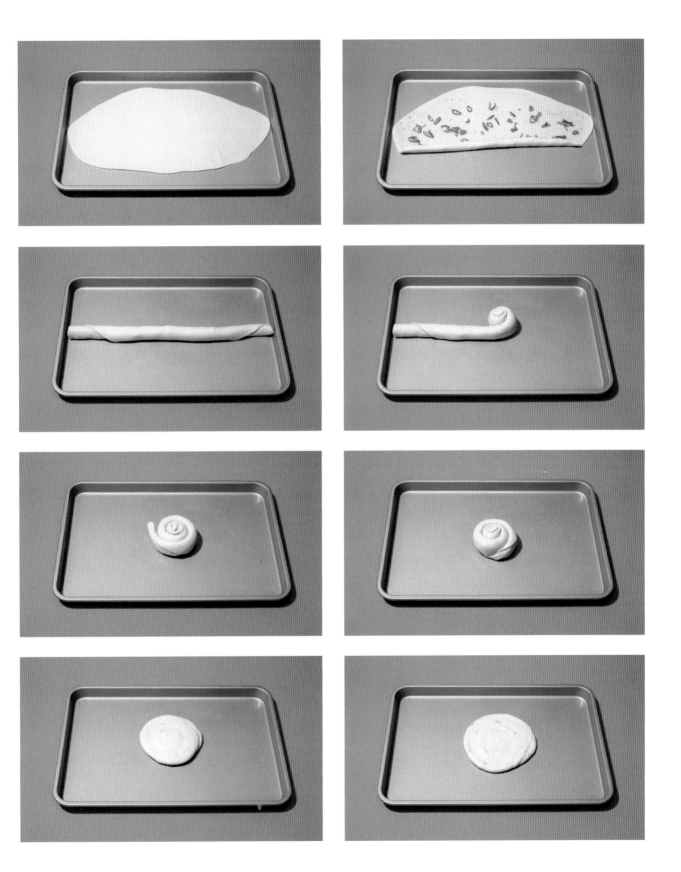

A Tale of Two Döners

I could never forgive myself if I didn't include döner kebab in this book—the signature street food of my hometown Berlin. If you're wondering how a Turkish dish ended up earning this title, I am not mad. Let me explain.

Döner kebab (which literally translates to "rotating grilled meat") did indeed originate as a convenience food in the Ottoman Empire. A wave of Turkish migrants who helped fuel Germany's rise as an economic powerhouse in the 1960s brought this tradition with them, and it did not take long for the first döner shops to start popping up across West Berlin and the Ruhr area, Germany's industrial "rust belt." Döner quickly became first a working-class favorite, then an icon of the bohemian Berlin lifestyle in the decades around the fall of the Berlin Wall. Nowadays, döner is a mainstream staple in German food culture.

But is it a Turkish dish? Its roots undisputedly are. But the iteration you find in Berlin has little to do with its Ottoman granddaddy. While I am sure someone has at some point done it before, stuffing the freshly grilled and sliced meat into a handheld bread pocket along with fresh vegetables was not a common practice in Türkiye; it was more often served with rice and salad on the side.

The particular combination of fresh vegetables (onions, red cabbage, shredded lettuce, diced cucumbers, and tomatoes) paired with a slathering of thick, sweet, mayo-forward sauce is also in stark contrast to the sparse veggie accompaniment with perhaps a drizzle of tahini yogurt and a dash of chili paste on the side that you'd get in Türkiye. It reflects local tastes as well as differences in ingredient supply.

While real-deal döner kebab, like a Viennese *schnitzel*, is explicitly made from veal, Berlin is home to what is unarguably a local creation: Berlin-style chicken döner. When Germany panicked over an outbreak of mad cow disease in the 1990s, the döner industry initially took a big hit. Smart local food entrepreneurs started producing chicken-based döner spits. (Nearly all shops in Berlin order prefabricated, frozen meat spits—you can catch them installing them around 10 a.m.) This move was meant to temporarily win back people's trust, and the plan worked. By the time consumers were ready to order veal again, the new option had already gained an enthusiastic following. Eventually, a slightly different style of kebab evolved around chicken döner, with a round roll, added fried veggies, crumbled feta, and a finish of lemon juice and soy sauce (or Maggi seasoning). The recipe in this book combines elements of both in an attempt to find the best version for your home cooking endeavors.

In short, there are plenty of reasons to argue that the döner you find in Germany is more than a bastardized version of a foreign dish. It's a true local innovation on a beloved classic. It is also a delicious monument to the indispensable role Turkish migrants played in the history of post-war Germany.

But aside from being a tasty meal, what did döner represent culturally for someone like me, a kid growing up in 1990s and 2000s Berlin? More than you could probably imagine. The fact that döner was dirt cheap (sometimes half the price of a pizza) made it so incredibly affordable, it was actually within budget for, say, a 12-year-old on his weekly pocket money. I would know, because I was that 12-year-old, along with my school friends. Döner was the first meal we could afford to buy for ourselves. Sure, we loved the MSG-fueled goodness, but it was also an act of emancipation. A ritual we'd engage in weekly, sometimes multiple times.

A few years later, döner would become an integral part of the post-partying experience. No drunken way home would be complete without a stop at the döner shop. I am to this day convinced it actually holds hangover-preventing properties—maybe it's the garlic.

And while a macro tracking Andong in his thirties is more conscious when it comes to his döner consumption, it will always have a place in my heart.

ANTI-PERFECTIONIST PAD THAI

SERVES
2

PREP TIME
15 minutes

COOK TIME
15 minutes

This pad thai is a lot tastier than it should be considering how easy it is to make. It will not hit all the flavor notes you'd expect in a 100 precent traditional pad thai, but the upshot is that you're unlikely to have difficulties sourcing the right tamarind paste or palm sugar. If you are as fascinated by this dish's history as I am, you know there is no need to worry about authenticity anyway!

DIRECTIONS

1. Cook the rice noodles according to package instructions until al dente. Set aside.

2. In a small bowl, whisk together the eggs and salt. Set aside.

3. To make the sauce, in a small bowl, whisk together all sauce ingredients until the sugar is mostly dissolved.

4. In a hot wok over medium-high heat, heat 1 tablespoon cooking oil until it ripples. Add the egg mixture and scramble for about 30 seconds or until soft curds form. Remove the eggs from the wok and set aside.

5. Wipe the wok clean. Add the remaining 2 tablespoons cooking oil and heat over medium-high heat until shimmering. Add the tofu and shrimp and stir-fry for about 90 seconds or until the shrimp are fully cooked and begin to brown. Add the ginger, garlic, and shallot. Stir for 30 seconds or until fragrant.

6. Add the noodles, scallions, bean sprouts, and scrambled eggs. Using a sturdy pair of chopsticks, briefly mix to combine.

7. Give the sauce one final stir, and pour over the sides of the wok. Mix to combine. Stir-fry for about 2 minutes or until the sauce has mostly been absorbed.

8. Divide between two serving plates and garnish with lime wedges, chili flakes, and roasted peanuts to taste.

7 oz (200g) dry **pad thai rice noodles**

2 large **eggs**

⅛ tsp **salt**

3 tbsp **neutral cooking oil,** divided

3 oz (100g) **firm tofu**

2 oz (75g) **medium shrimp,** peeled and deveined

1-inch (2.5cm) piece **fresh ginger,** chopped

3 cloves **garlic,** sliced

1 **shallot,** minced

3 **scallions,** light and dark green parts only, thinly sliced on the bias

2 cups **bean sprouts** (4.2oz / 120g), loosely packed

FOR THE SAUCE

3 tbsp **fish sauce**

3 tbsp **lime juice**

2 tbsp **soy sauce**

1½ tbsp **dark soy sauce**

3 tbsp **brown sugar**

FOR GARNISH

2 **lime wedges**

1 tsp **red chili flakes**

¼ cup **roasted peanuts**

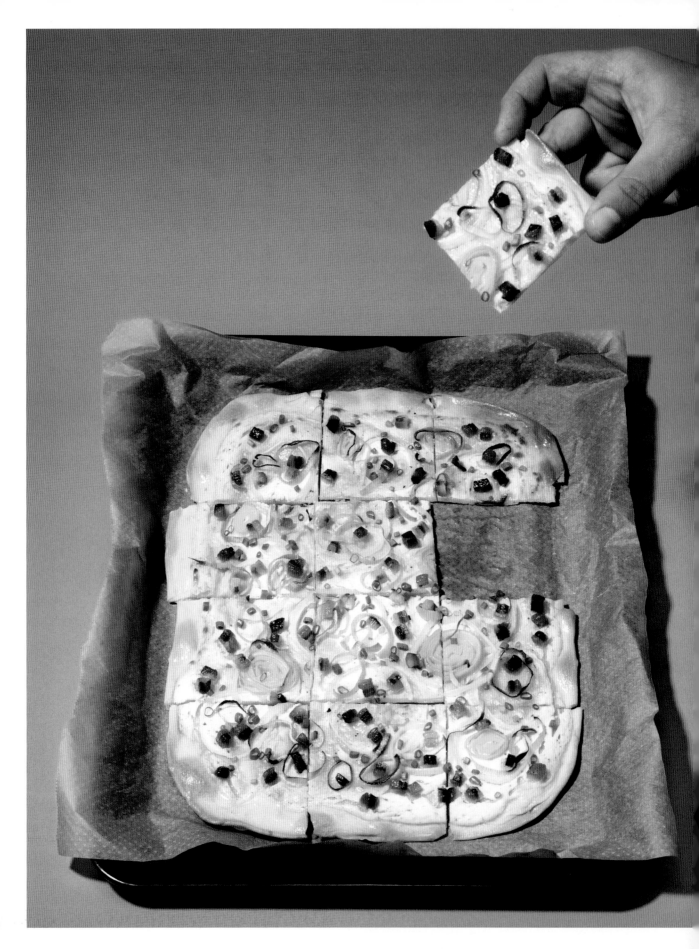

FLAMMKUCHEN

SERVES
4

PREP TIME
20 minutes + 35 minutes inactive time

COOK TIME
12 minutes

Flammkuchen is the Franco-German answer to pizza. And while many would argue it's a totally different thing altogether (and I wouldn't fully disagree), it's a dream for home cooks. Since the dough is not yeasted, there are no long proofing times and you can simply roll it out—already a game changer. Next time you're craving DIY pizza, try flammkuchen and you might never go back.

DIRECTIONS

1. In a large bowl, combine flour, salt, oil, and water. Mix until all ingredients come together as a cohesive dough with no dry flour remaining. Cover and rest for 15 minutes.

2. Knead for 5 minutes until a smooth dough comes together. Cover and rest another 20 minutes. Meanwhile, preheat the oven to 450°F (230°C) and line a baking sheet with parchment paper.

3. In a small bowl, mix the sour cream, salt, pepper, and nutmeg. Set aside.

4. Lightly dust a work surface with flour. Roll out the dough as thinly as possible, roughly to the size of your baking sheet. Lightly dust the dough with flour. Carefully roll it up, transfer to the prepared baking sheet, and unroll.

5. With the back of a spoon, spread the sour cream mixture over the dough. Evenly spread the onion, leeks, and ham over the sour cream.

6. Place in the oven on the lowest rack, and bake for 8 to 12 minutes until the crust is crispy and the edges are brown. Cut into 12 pieces and serve immediately.

1¼ cups **bread flour** (5.5oz / 150g)

½ tsp **salt**

1 tbsp **neutral cooking oil** (0.5oz / 15g)

2½ oz (70g) **water**

FOR THE TOPPING

1 cup **sour cream** (about 25% fat content)

¼ tsp **salt**

½ tsp freshly cracked **black pepper** (20 cracks)

2 pinches of freshly grated **nutmeg**

½ **yellow onion,** thinly sliced

2 medium **leeks,** white and tender green parts only, thinly sliced

5 oz (140g) **dry-cured ham** or **bacon,** diced

CUBAN SANDWICH, GERMANIZED

SERVES
2

PREP TIME
5 minutes

COOK TIME
10 minutes

I first tried a Cuban sandwich on a trip to Miami, and I immediately fell in love. (If you've never had this pressed ham-and-cheese masterpiece, what are you waiting for?) Making an authentic Cuban version from scratch can take days, but I realized that all the traditional ingredients could be replaced with items that are local to Berlin. The result is a mind-blowing Germanized version. This is your friendly reminder to play around with local ingredients!

DIRECTIONS

1. Slice each pretzel in half lengthwise. For both pretzels, spread 1 tablespoon mayo on the bottom half and ½ tablespoon mustard on the top half.

2. Top the bottom halves with ham, roast pork, cheese, and pickles. Close each sandwich.

3. Grill each sandwich in a sandwich press for 3 to 4 minutes or until the cheese has melted. (See note.)

4. Immediately rub the top side of the bread with the garlic clove and brush with softened butter. Cut in half and enjoy.

NOTE: If you don't have a sandwich press, use a large cast-iron skillet on medium heat. Cover the sandwich with parchment paper and place a second heavy skillet or stock pot filled with water on top to press the sandwich down. After 2 minutes, flip and repeat for the second side.

2 large soft **pretzel breadsticks** or **pretzel buns**

2 tbsp **mayonnaise**

1 tbsp **Bavarian sweet mustard**

6 slices **Kassler** or **ham**, medium thickness

6 slices **roast pork**, medium thickness

4 slices **Emmental cheese**

2 **sour pickles**, sliced lengthwise into planks

1 tbsp softened **butter**

1 large clove **garlic**, halved lengthwise

FORBIDDEN CHOW MEIN

SERVES
2
PREP TIME
10 minutes
COOK TIME
20 minutes

Chow mein was one of my first Chinese food obsessions. While the traditional versions are still my gold standard, I started playing around with fusing Italian pasta shapes with basic chow mein ingredients. Outrageous, I know—but it works. It works frighteningly well. Find out if you agree!

DIRECTIONS

1. In a pot of boiling water, cook the pasta according to package instructions until al dente. Drain and set aside.

2. To make the sauce, in a small bowl, combine the soy sauce, oyster sauce, sugar, sesame oil, salt, MSG, and garlic. Mix well and set aside.

3. In a wok, heat the oil over medium-high heat until it ripples. Add the chicken and stir-fry for about 1 minute or until lightly browned.

4. Add the onion and stir-fry for 1 minute or until fragrant. Add the carrot and white parts of the scallions and stir-fry for 1 minute more. Add the cooked pasta and bean sprouts and stir-fry for about 1 minute.

5. Give the sauce a quick stir and add it to the wok. Cook for 1 minute more, stirring continuously. Turn off the heat and add the butter. Stir until the butter is completely melted.

6. Transfer to serving plates and garnish with the green part of the scallions. Eat with a spoon for extra inauthenticity.

9 oz (250g) **orecchiette**

2 tbsp **neutral cooking oil**

7 oz (200g) cooked **chicken breast,** diced

½ **yellow onion,** diced

1 **carrot,** diced

3 **scallions,** sliced, light and dark green parts divided

2 cups **bean sprouts** (4.2oz / 120g), loosely packed

1 tbsp cold **butter**

FOR THE SAUCE

2 tbsp **soy sauce**

1 tbsp **oyster sauce**

1 tsp **granulated sugar**

½ tsp **sesame oil**

½ tsp **salt**

¼ tsp **MSG**

½ small clove **garlic,** minced

Midday Meals

Picking the right lunchtime meal can be surprisingly difficult. It should probably not take all day, and it shouldn't be a meal that makes you fall into a food coma (which usually lasts until dinnertime). This chapter is a collection of my favorite recipes for this most fleeting meal of the day.

Baba Ganoush **123**

Chutagi **125**

Hand-Pulled Noodles **127**

Easy Hummus with Toppings **129**
    Feta, Mango & Chili Topping **130**
    Smoky Paprika Yogurt Topping **130**
    Spicy Beef Crumble Topping **131**
    Zesty Pesto Topping **131**

Coca-Cola Chicken Wings **133**

Fusion Cheesy Garlic Noodles **134**

Chinese Turnip Cake **138**

Falafel Fried Rice **141**

Pasta e Fagioli **142**

Tomato Fried Eggs **145**

Midday Meals: It's All About Balance

Close your eyes and imagine your ideal lunch. Where do you find yourself? Near a bustling Middle Eastern sukh? A cozy restaurant in a sleepy Tuscan village? Or maybe a classic Cantonese dim sum shop? Good news—I have recipes for you from all of the above.

THE LEVANT: A LUNCHTIME PARADISE

First and foremost, lunch makes me think of Levantine cuisine, specifically **hummus.** It's a fantastic earlier-in-the-day meal—and is, in fact, traditionally seen as such. My favorite places in Berlin are open only during breakfast and lunch hours, a practice I also witnessed in both Palestinian- and Jewish-run hummus shops in Israel. To my taste, a plate of velvety, creamy spread with a side of fresh or pickled veggies as dipping vehicles is the sweet spot for lunch.

I know people who don't get the hype around hummus, and I understand. To me, this is about setting the right expectations. Even the best hummus will still be hummus. You just need to appreciate it for what it is: a relatively mild tasting and texturally pleasing dish you either love for this very reason, or you go heavy on the aforementioned Lebanese pickles and olives on the side. (Also, name one person that dips a big slice of raw onion into hummus and calls it bland).

Then there is **baba ganoush.** This creamy eggplant spread makes an excellent side dish and can be a culinary crowd-pleaser when done right. The secret is in keeping it smoky as well as balancing fattiness and acidity—an elaborate interplay between yogurt, lemon juice, and, indeed, mayo. Add it to any carb and protein and you have yourself a texturally balanced meal.

AROUND THE WORLD IN FOUR PASTA DISHES

Another lunchtime classic—pasta. You just can't go wrong with pasta. If you like the Italian kind, I have a recipe for you: **pasta e fagioli.** If you have never had this before, the thought of putting beans in pasta might not sound like a great idea. But wait until you've tried it!

More a fan of chewy, fresh Chinese-style noodles? Maybe even the hand-pulled kind? Do not fret. There are different types of **hand-pulled noodles,** and this recipe is definitely beginner friendly.

If, like me, you often can't decide between Italian or Asian noodles—why not have the best of both worlds? Over in California, Vietnamese American restaurateurs did just that, creating one of the area's unofficial signature dishes: **fusion cheesy garlic noodles.**

Even further off the beaten path, in a remote corner of the Himalayas, people love noodles. On a trip to beautiful Ladakh, I first got to try **chutagi,** a simple dish of noodles that bring to mind Italian orecchiette in shape and are cooked in a delicious, lightly curried broth.

I EXERCISE FOR EXTRA RICE

As much as I love pasta, there is something deeply satisfying about rice. I could simply not last more than a few days without it, and I usually have a little tub with precooked rice in the fridge—because you never know when that fried rice craving might hit. And we all know fried rice is best made from day-old rice. Or is it?

There is another way, usually known as the "pilaf method." You briefly roast dry rice in a bit of oil before adding water. The result is a texture somewhere between steamed rice and fried rice, leaning toward the latter. Not just a convenient and time-saving technique, but also a great way to layer in more flavor

during the cooking process—just follow my **falafel fried rice** recipe, and you'll see what I mean.

You can keep it even simpler and make an "over-rice dish." That's an actual term in China for a roughly defined category of saucy recipes that are usually quick and easy to whip up. Probably the most common among them, **tomato fried eggs.** Optimized for canned tomatoes, the version in this book might be even easier than the already straightforward classic.

And since we are in the realm of Chinese cuisine, one of the best things I could possibly imagine for lunch is dim sum. Yes, most dim sum dishes are out of reach for the casual home cook. But if there is one you wanna add to your repertoire to freeze and get out for the occasional teatime with a twist, my recommendation would 100 percent be **Chinese turnip cake.**

BABA GANOUSH

SERVES
2

PREP TIME
15 minutes

COOK TIME
60 minutes

The perfect side dish exists, and it's baba ganoush! It makes a rich meal lighter and a light meal richer. Smoky, tangy, and creamy at once, this recipe is easy to prepare in advance and works as a spread, dip, or sauce.

DIRECTIONS

1. Preheat the oven to 400°F (200°C) and line a baking sheet with parchment paper. Using a fork, pierce the eggplants three times on each side. Place on the prepared baking sheet, and roast for 60 minutes. Once cool enough to handle, cut each eggplant in half lengthwise. Using a spoon, scoop the flesh into a bowl.

2. In a food processor, combine the yogurt, lemon juice, tahini, garlic, cumin, paprika, and salt. Blend for about 20 seconds or until homogeneous. Add the roasted eggplant and mayonnaise, if using. Blend for 20 seconds more until well combined, with just a few small chunks remaining.

3. Serve immediately or refrigerate for at least 4 hours to chill. To serve, spread on a serving plate and top with olive oil, parsley, and smoked paprika.

3 medium **eggplants**
(2lb / 1kg in total)

½ cup **plain Greek yogurt**
(5.3oz / 150g)

¼ cup **lemon juice** (1.8oz / 50g)

⅓ cup **tahini** (3.5oz / 100g)

1 clove **garlic,** finely minced

½ tsp **ground cumin**

¼–½ tsp **smoked paprika**

1 tsp **salt**

1 tbsp **mayonnaise** (optional)

TO SERVE

2–3 tbsp **olive oil**

3 sprigs **fresh parsley,** leaves
only, finely minced

½ tsp **smoked paprika**

CHUTAGI
(LADAKHI NOODLE STEW)

SERVES
4

PREP TIME
15 minutes

COOK TIME
40 minutes

It's safe to say that Ladakh, the northernmost part of India, was one of the most remote places I got to see. Located high up in the Himalayan mountains, it's blessed with breathtaking mountain views—but also a traditionally very limited supply of ingredients to cook with. During the brief summers though, Ladakhis love cooking this hearty veggie soup with handmade noodles—so here it is!

DIRECTIONS

1. To make the dough, in a medium bowl, combine the flour, salt, water, and sesame oil. Mix and lightly knead for 5 minutes until a rough ball is formed. Cover with a damp towel and set aside.

2. Bring a large saucepan to medium heat, add oil and sweat the onion for 1 minute. Add the garlic and ginger and mix well. Add the mustard and fennel seeds, and sauté for 1 minute. Add the turmeric, cayenne, and cumin, and stir for 20 seconds.

3. Add the potatoes, carrot, and radishes, and stir-fry for 2 to 3 minutes. Add the water, canned tomatoes, and salt. Simmer over medium heat for 30 minutes. Add more water if the liquid level sinks noticeably below the starting amount.

4. Meanwhile, lightly dust a work surface with flour. Turn out the dough and knead it briefly. Divide the dough into three pieces of equal size and roll each piece into a rope roughly ¾ inch (1–2cm) in diameter. Cut or pinch off small almond-sized nuggets. Lightly dust each nugget with flour, then flatten by using your thumb to press the dough into small disks the size of a coin.

5. Once the stew has been simmering for 30 minutes, add the dumplings, frozen peas, and spinach. Cook for 3 to 5 minutes or until the dumplings are cooked al dente. Serve garnished with diced tomato, shallot, and cilantro to taste.

2 tbsp **neutral cooking oil**

1 large **red onion**, diced

2 cloves **garlic**, minced

1-inch (2.5cm) piece **fresh ginger**, minced

1 tsp **mustard seeds**

1 tsp **fennel seeds**

2 tsp **turmeric powder**

2 tsp **cayenne** or **paprika**

1 tsp **ground cumin**

2 medium **potatoes**, diced

1 medium **carrot**, diced

3 **radishes**, diced (optional)

4½ cups (1L) **water**

1 8 ½ oz (240g) can **crushed tomatoes**

2 tsp **salt**

½ cup **frozen peas**

1 cup **frozen spinach**

FOR THE DOUGH

7 oz (200g) **whole wheat flour**

½ tsp **salt**

½ cup **water** (4oz / 115g)

½ tsp **toasted sesame oil**

TO SERVE

1 **tomato**, diced (optional)

1 **shallot**, thinly sliced

HAND-PULLED NOODLES
WITH CHILI SOY DRESSING

SCAN FOR VIDEO

SERVES
2

PREP TIME
10 minutes + 90 minutes to
4 hours inactive time

COOK TIME
20 minutes

Pulling noodles by hand requires years of practice? Not with this method! In fact, this might be one of the easiest fresh pasta recipes out there. Topped with an addictive chili soy dressing that can be whipped up in minutes, this is your gateway into the world of homemade Chinese noodles.

2 cups (250g) **all-purpose flour**

½ tsp **salt**

½ cups + 1 tbsp **water**
(4.6oz / 130g)

½ tbsp **neutral cooking oil**

FOR TOPPING

1 tbsp **soy sauce**

1 tbsp **dark Chinese vinegar**

½ tsp **sesame oil**

¼ tsp **salt**

½ tsp **granulated sugar**

1 cup **mung bean sprouts,**
packed

2 tbsp finely chopped **fresh
cilantro** (optional)

2 tbsp minced **scallions**

1 tsp minced **garlic**

1 tsp ground **Sichuan pepper**

2 tsp **red chili flakes**

3 tbsp **neutral cooking oil**

DIRECTIONS

1. In a large bowl, whisk together the flour and salt. Add the water and roughly knead into a ball until no dry flour remains. It should feel firm but pliable. Cover and rest for 45 minutes.

2. Knead the rested dough for about 1 minute. Shape into a ball. Using a rolling pin, flatten the ball into a thick disk (roughly 7 inches [20cm] in diameter). Cover with an upside-down bowl and rest for 3 minutes.

3. Spread the oil in a 7 x 10-inch (20 x 27cm) baking dish, coating the bottom and sides of the dish. Transfer the dough to the oiled baking dish. Using your hands, flatten and spread it until it covers the whole dish. Flip around to make sure it is well oiled on both sides. Cover with plastic wrap and rest for at least 30 minutes or up to 4 hours.

4. Carefully transfer the dough to a large cutting board. With a large chef's knife, slice the dough into ½-inch (1.25cm) strips. (Scan QR code for video instruction.)

5. Prepare a large pot filled with simmering water over medium high heat. Take each noodle and gently pull until it is roughly 3 feet (1m) long and less than ¼ inch (5mm) thick. Drop into the hot water. Work one at a time until all the noodles are in the water. Cook for 1 minute more. Drain the noodles and rinse under running cold water for about 5 seconds.

6. Divide the noodles evenly between two serving bowls. Into each bowl, add half of the soy sauce, vinegar, sesame oil, salt, and sugar.

7. To each serving, add a small handful of bean sprouts and top with half of the cilantro (if using), scallions, garlic, Sichuan pepper, and chili flakes.

8. In a small saucepan over high heat, heat the oil until you see the first wisp of smoke. Quickly and carefully pour half the oil over each serving, trying to hit most of the chili flakes, garlic, and scallions. Serve and stir well before eating.

EASY HUMMUS
WITH TOPPINGS

SERVES
4

PREP TIME
5 minutes

COOK TIME
10 minutes

Hummus can be a science, but it doesn't have to be. This recipe can be on the table in less than 15 minutes, and it does the job very well. If you ask me, hummus really shines when you add the right toppings. From rich and savory to light and tangy—you've got plenty of options from which to choose.

1 lb (450g) **canned chickpeas,** drained and rinsed

⅓ cup **water** (3oz / 85g)

½ cup **plain Greek yogurt** (4.2oz / 120g)

⅓ cup **tahini** (3oz / 85g)

1 clove **garlic**

2 tbsp **lemon juice** (0.9oz / 25g)

½ tsp **ground cumin**

1 tsp **salt**

2 tbsp **extra virgin olive oil** (0.9oz / 25g)

DIRECTIONS

1. In a medium saucepan, combine the chickpeas and water. Bring to a boil over medium-high heat, then reduce heat and simmer for 2 to 3 minutes.

2. In a food processor, blend the yogurt, tahini, garlic, lemon juice, cumin, and salt until homogeneous.

3. Add the hot chickpeas with their cooking liquid to the food processor and blend for 2 minutes or until smooth.

4. Add the oil and blend for 2 to 3 minutes more or until smooth and creamy. Thin with 1 to 3 tablespoons of water, if desired.

5. Enjoy immediately, or transfer to an airtight container and refrigerate. Hummus can be stored for up to 5 days. If desired, serve with one of the four hummus topping options (pages 130–131).

HUMMUS TOPPING:
FETA, MANGO & CHILI

SERVES
2

PREP TIME
5 minutes

COOK TIME
None

DIRECTIONS

1. In a small bowl, toss the mango with the salt, chili flakes, olive oil, and cilantro leaves.

2. To serve, top hummus with the spiced mango mixture. Crumble feta on top.

½ **mango** (2oz / 50g), finely diced

Small pinch of **salt**

½ tsp **red chili flakes**

1 tbsp **extra virgin olive oil**

3 sprigs **fresh cilantro**, leaves only, minced

2 oz (50g) **feta**

HUMMUS TOPPING:
SMOKY PAPRIKA YOGURT

SERVES
2

PREP TIME
5 minutes

COOK TIME
5 minutes

DIRECTIONS

1. In a small saucepan on medium heat, melt the butter with the smoked paprika for about 1 minute or until the butter is fully melted and starts to bubble.

2. To serve, spread a layer of yogurt over hummus and drizzle the infused butter on top. Garnish with jalapeño slices and sumac.

1 oz (30g) **butter**

½ tsp **smoked paprika**

2½ oz (75g) **plain yogurt**

1 **jalapeño**, sliced

¼ tsp **ground sumac**

HUMMUS TOPPING:
SPICY BEEF CRUMBLE

SERVES	2
PREP TIME	5 minutes
COOK TIME	10 minutes

DIRECTIONS

1. In a small skillet, heat the oil over medium high heat until it shimmers. Add the beef, and break it into crumbles using a spatula.

2. Stir in the salt, chili flakes, cumin, and cinnamon. Cook for 3 to 5 minutes or until the beef is browned and crispy.

3. To serve, spread the spiced beef over hummus and garnish with parsley.

1 tbsp **neutral cooking oil**
4 oz (100g) **ground beef**
¼ tsp **salt**
½ tsp **red chili flakes**
¼ tsp **ground cumin**
⅛ tsp **ground cinnamon**
2 tbsp chopped **fresh parsley**

HUMMUS TOPPING:
ZESTY PESTO

SERVES	2
PREP TIME	5 minutes
COOK TIME	3 minutes

DIRECTIONS

1. In a medium skillet, toast the pine nuts over medium heat for 2 to 3 minutes or until golden brown. Stir frequently to prevent burning. Set aside 1 tablespoon toasted pine nuts.

2. To a small food processor, add 2 tablespoons pine nuts, garlic, parsley, olive oil, lemon juice and zest, chili flakes, and salt. Process until homogeneous. (Alternatively, you can use a mortar and pestle.)

3. To serve, top hummus with the pesto and garnish with the reserved pine nuts.

3 tbsp **pine nuts**
½ clove **garlic**
¼ cup **fresh parsley**, packed
2 tbsp **extra virgin olive oil**
2 tbsp **lemon juice**
Zest of ¼ **lemon**
½ tsp **red chili flakes**
⅛ tsp **salt**

COCA-COLA CHICKEN WINGS

SERVES
2

PREP TIME
5 minutes

COOK TIME
35 minutes

It has become almost tradition in China that this is one of the first dishes people learn to cook by themselves, thanks to the magic ingredient: cola. The addition of soy sauce turns it into an instant sweet-and-savory flavor bomb that only improves when you reduce it to a glaze.

DIRECTIONS

1. Separate the chicken wings into the drumettes and wingettes. Discard the wing tips or reserve for stock.

2. Coat a large, cold nonstick skillet evenly with cooking oil and place the chicken in a single layer, flat side down. Place the skillet over medium-high heat and brown the wings on one side for 8 to 10 minutes or until the bottoms are golden and they release from the pan without much sticking.

3. Meanwhile, in a medium bowl, stir together the cola, soy sauce, honey, and oyster sauce.

4. Decrease the heat on the chicken to medium. Drain the fat from the skillet, leaving the chicken in the pan. Add the cola sauce, ginger, and garlic. Cover and simmer for 2 minutes.

5. Flip the wings and scrape up any bits of meat that may have stuck to the pan. Simmer for 25 minutes until the sauce is thick enough to leave a streak when you run a spatula through it.

6. Remove the ginger and garlic chunks and discard. Toss the wings in the pan and coat evenly in the sauce.

7. Remove the wings from the skillet and garnish with cilantro, scallions, and sesame seeds, to taste. Serve with rice, if desired.

1⅓ lb (600g) **chicken wings** (about 4 wings)

¼ cup **neutral cooking oil**

½ cup original **Coca-Cola** or other nondiet **cola** (4oz / 120g)

2 tbsp **soy sauce**

1 tbsp **honey**

1 tbsp **oyster sauce**

1-inch (2.5cm) piece **fresh ginger,** roughly sliced and crushed

3 cloves **garlic,** peeled and bruised

Steamed **white rice** (optional), to serve

TO GARNISH
Chopped **fresh cilantro**

Sliced **scallions**

Toasted **sesame seeds**

FUSION CHEESY GARLIC NOODLES

SERVES
2

PREP TIME
5 minutes

COOK TIME
20 minutes

Everything you love about a cheesy pasta dish, but with that extra umami kick you can typically only find in the cuisines of Asia. It's only a matter of time until this modern classic from San Francisco conquers the world. Be ahead of the curve and try it tonight!

DIRECTIONS

1. Bring a large pot of salted water to a boil, and cook the pasta according to the package instructions until just shy of al dente. Drain and set aside.

2. Meanwhile, in a small bowl, stir together the soy sauce, oyster sauce, fish sauce, MSG, and ¼ cup water.

3. In a wok over medium-high heat, add olive oil. Add the garlic and sauté for 30 seconds or until fragrant. Add cooked pasta and stir. Add the sauce and cook, stirring occasionally, for 1 minute.

4. Turn off the heat and add the Parmesan, butter, and the remaining ¼ cup water. Stir until fully incorporated and creamy.

5. Divide between two serving plates and garnish with parsley, chives, or ½ tablespoon Chimichurri (page 221), as desired.

9 oz (250g) **spaghetti**

1 tbsp **soy sauce** (0.5oz / 15g)

1 tbsp **oyster sauce** (0.5oz / 15g)

1 tbsp **fish sauce** (0.5oz / 15g)

¼ tsp **MSG**

½ cup **water**, divided

2 tbsp **olive oil**

5 cloves **garlic**, finely minced

½ cup grated **Parmesan cheese** (1.8oz / 50g)

1 tbsp cold **butter** (0.5oz / 15g)

1 tbsp finely chopped **fresh parsley** (optional), to garnish

1 tbsp finely chopped **fresh chives** (optional), to garnish

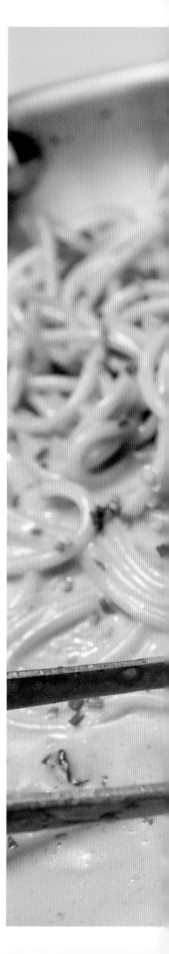

A Love Letter to the Workday Lunch

Before I started my first job, I always imagined that workday lunches would involve awkward, lackluster conversations among people wearing suits, talking over the logistics of a project they don't really care about. I might not have been far off, in some cases, but I would never have guessed that for a whole year, workday lunches would become my favorite part of the day.

Let me take you back to a November day in Shanghai. I had just graduated university and moved to the city. Wearing my best business-casual attire, I was on my way to work. I was sweating. A November day in Shanghai was much warmer than what I was used to. But also, it was my first day on the job working as a video producer for a cutting-edge social media marketing agency, and I was about to meet my new bosses and colleagues.

In spite of having a bit of a language barrier, the first meetings went well. It was all polite and professional, and the company's IT admin helped me set up my workstation. When he was introduced to me as *Pangzi*, literally Chinese for "fatso," I first thought it must be my shaky Mandarin and I heard wrong. I mean, he was a heavier gentleman, but come on. Well, they really did call him fatso, and he was more than fine with it. At least for men, being fat does not carry a negative connotation in Chinese culture, Pangzi explained to me with a big, charming grin on his face.

Once my computer was set up and I began working on my first, very basic assignment by myself, the situation started sinking in. There I was, the only European in a company with 80 Chinese employees who barely spoke English. How would I manage to communicate with clients and colleagues, or live up to my bosses' expectations? And maybe more importantly, would I ever manage to connect with my coworkers socially? A fear of being isolated started creeping in. Fortunately, I had my extremely basic assignment to distract me.

Just moments after the clock struck 12, I started hearing some rumbling around me. In my experience, lunchtime was sacred for many in China; it had to be 12 p.m. on the dot. As the first small groups of coworkers were leaving the office to go out for a snack, there it was again, that fear of being left out. I could already see myself getting a steamed bun at the local 7-Eleven and spending my lunch break all alone watching YouTube videos on my work computer, when I suddenly heard a voice over my shoulder. "Andong, you coming?" It was the company's lead designer, a tall and handsome guy with a thick Shanghai accent. "Come on," he said and turned around, playing it cool. I quickly grabbed my jacket and followed him outside, where a small group of colleagues from the creative department were waiting for us.

Our office was located in a newly built and pretty soulless part of town full of office buildings and construction sites for more office buildings. That first day, my colleagues took me to a noodle place run by a former chef from China's People's Liberation Army—a man who knew exactly how to feed large groups of people. How he managed to serve steaming hot but not overcooked noodles mere moments after we ordered will forever remain a mystery to me.

The lunch we had that day initially felt a bit distant and awkward, just the way I had imagined it. We all weren't quite sure if we should talk about work, the news, or our private lives. But I didn't care. All I could feel was a deep sense of gratitude for not having to eat a steamed bun while watching videos all by myself. Eventually, IT admin Pangzi broke the ice when he, much to everyone's amusement, ordered a second bowl of noodles before most of us even started eating our first. It was a decent lunch in culinary terms, but an excellent time for an anxious Andong trying to connect to his surroundings in an entirely new culture.

And with that, a new ritual was born. Every day, I was eagerly waiting for the clock to strike 12 to hear my designer colleague call for me: "Andong, you coming?" Another day, another lunch. We ended up becoming close friends. Some lunches we would spend with our colleagues, some just between the two of us.

It's funny how quickly cultural and language barriers can disappear when you go through the same things with someone. We shared the same projects, clients, bosses, and coworkers. Eventually, we talked about family and relationships, about dreams, ambitions, and frustrations. There was always something to talk about. And it was always over a quickly served bowl of never great (but also never terrible) lunch—the best part of my day, the one I could always look forward to.

CHINESE TURNIP CAKE
(LUO BO GAO)

MAKES
12 pieces

PREP TIME
20 minutes

COOK TIME
1 hour 20 minutes + 2 hours to cool

Lou bo gao is perhaps the most underrated dim sum order of all time—at least outside of China, where turnip cake is a classic on Lunar New Year and all year round. Once you get the hang of this dish, it can also be your blank canvas for a whole new world of "rice cakes"!

DIRECTIONS

1. Place the shiitake and shrimp in a small bowl. Add boiling water to cover and let sit for at least 20 minutes. Once fully rehydrated, discard the soaking water, remove mushroom stems, and finely dice both the shiitake and shrimp. Set aside.

2. Preheat the oven to 350°F (180°C). Line a 9 x 13-inch (20 x 35cm) baking dish with parchment paper. (See note.)

3. To a cold wok or large sauté pan, add the cooking oil and lap cheong. Cook over medium heat for 5 minutes, stirring occasionally, until the fat has rendered and the sausage begins to crisp. Add the onion, shiitake, and shrimp. Stir-fry for 3 minutes or until the ingredients begin to crackle and pop. Transfer the contents of the wok to a plate and set aside. Wipe the pan clean.

4. To the same pan, add the radish, water, sugar, ½ teaspoon salt, and MSG. Cover and simmer over medium heat for 5 minutes until the radish has softened.

5. Meanwhile, to make the slurry, whisk together all ingredients in a small bowl.

6. Once the radish has softened, return the sausage, mushroom, shrimp, and onion mixture to the pan. Give the slurry a quick stir and add it to the pan. Start stirring immediately. Within 2 to 3 minutes, the slurry will turn into a very thick and slightly translucent paste. Keep stirring gently to ensure it doesn't burn. Once the mixture has fully gelled up, remove it from the heat.

7. Transfer the mixture to the prepared baking dish. Wet your hands and spread the mixture around to evenly fill the dish. (Be careful; the mixture may still be quite hot.) With a wet rubber spatula, smooth the surface. Sprinkle sesame seeds evenly over top.

8. Cover the baking dish with foil, sealing the edges as well as you can. Bake for 45 minutes or until the internal temperature registers at least 195°F (90°C).

9. Remove from the oven and let cool for 10 minutes. Remove the foil, transfer to a cooling rack, and let cool completely for at least 2 hours or—even better—in the fridge overnight. Cut into 12 pieces before panfrying.

4 **dried shiitake mushrooms**

2 oz (50g) **dried shrimp**

1 tbsp **neutral cooking oil**

4 links **lap cheong sausage** (6.5oz / 180g), finely diced (see note)

1 **yellow onion**, finely diced

1 **daikon radish** (1.75lb / 800g), peeled and grated or finely diced

¾ cup + 2 tbsp **water** (200ml)

½ tbsp **granulated sugar**

1 tsp **salt**, divided

½ tsp **MSG**

½ cup **sesame seeds**

FOR THE SLURRY

1¼ cups cold **water** (10fl oz / 300ml)

½ cup **rice flour** (7oz / 200g)

¾ cup **tapioca starch** (3.5oz / 100g)

1 tsp **garlic powder**

½ tsp **ground white pepper**

½ tsp **five spice powder**

1 tsp **toasted sesame oil**

TO SERVE

3 tbsp **neutral cooking oil**

Chopped **scallions** or **fresh cilantro**, for garnish

¼ cup **Chinkiang** or **dark rice vinegar**

1 tbsp **soy sauce**

10. To serve, heat the oil in a nonstick frying pan over medium heat. When hot, add the pieces of turnip cake, sesame seed side down, and cook for 3 to 5 minutes. Flip and cook for 3 to 5 minutes more. Garnish with scallions or cilantro. To make a simple dipping sauce, combine the Chinkiang and soy sauce.

NOTES: When lining a baking dish with parchment paper, I like to use the following method: crumple up a sheet into a ball first, then unfold. The parchment paper will become a lot more pliable and easily stay in shape.

Lap cheong is a sweet Chinese sausage with a unique flavor profile. It is often available in Asian supermarkets. If you can't find it, substitute for the same amount of salsiccia or dry-cured country ham, which you season with ½ teaspoon five spice powder and 2 teaspoons honey after it has crisped up in the pan.

FALAFEL FRIED RICE

SERVES	2
PREP TIME	10 minutes
COOK TIME	30 minutes

What if you took all the flavors you love in falafel balls and turned them into a simple fried rice dish? This recipe is the result of an experiment that started on a whim but turned out so well, I included it in a video. These days it's a weeknight favorite not just in my house but for countless enthusiastic viewers of my channel, too.

DIRECTIONS

1. In a large nonstick skillet, sauté the onion in 2 tablespoons oil over medium-high heat for 3 minutes or until it begins to brown.

2. Add the garlic, cumin, coriander, cardamom, and chickpeas. Stir until combined. Sauté for 2 to 3 minutes or until the garlic begins to brown.

3. Add the rice, remaining 1 tablespoon oil, and salt. Stir until the rice is evenly coated in the spice mix. Toast for 1 to 2 minutes.

4. Add the water. (Be careful; it might bubble up a bit.) Stir well and cover tightly with a lid. Cook for 2 minutes.

5. Reduce the heat to low. Cook for 20 minutes, covered, or until the rice has absorbed the liquid.

6. Meanwhile, prepare the sauce. In a small bowl, mix all ingredients until well combined. Set aside until ready to serve.

7. When the rice is cooked, remove the lid and stir in the chopped parsley, mint, and cilantro.

8. To serve, drizzle with tahini sauce and sriracha to taste. Garnish with paprika and cilantro, if desired.

½ **yellow onion,** diced

3 tbsp **olive oil,** divided

2 cloves **garlic,** minced

1 tsp **ground cumin**

1 tsp **ground coriander**

½ tsp **ground green cardamom**

7 oz (200g) **canned chickpeas,** rinsed and drained

1 cup **short-grain white rice** (6.5oz / 185g), thoroughly rinsed

½ tsp **salt**

1¾ cups **water** (14oz / 400g)

4 sprigs **fresh parsley,** finely chopped

4 sprigs **fresh mint,** finely chopped

4 sprigs **fresh cilantro,** finely chopped

FOR THE SAUCE

1½ tbsp **tahini** (0.8oz / 23g)

2 tsp **water**

½ cup **plain yogurt** (4.2oz / 120g)

⅛ tsp **salt**

TO SERVE

Sriracha or hot sauce

Paprika or smoked paprika (optional)

Chopped **fresh cilantro** (optional)

PASTA E FAGIOLI

SERVES

2

PREP TIME

10 minutes

COOK TIME

20 minutes

I once had an Italian roommate named Francesco, a very passionate home cook from Naples. He loved to share his cooking with his flatmates, and I learned so much about pasta from him. This recipe was one of his favorites, and rightfully so! Cheesy, creamy, filling, and on your plate in less than half an hour—I am never disappointed to go for this classic.

DIRECTIONS

1. In a large pot of boiling water, cook the pasta according to package instructions until almost al dente. Drain and set aside.

2. In a wok or large skillet, heat the olive oil over medium-high heat. Add the shallot and garlic, and saute for about 1 minute or until fragrant. Add the beans and stir-fry for 30 seconds. Add ¼ cup water, salt, and MSG. Bring to a simmer, and boil until the water has almost completely disappeared, about 2 to 3 minutes.

3. Add the wine and simmer for 2 minutes more. As it cooks, roughly mash the beans until only a few are left intact.

4. Reduce the heat to low and add the pasta. Stir until the sauce is evenly incorporated. Stir in the remaining ¼ cup water. Turn off the heat and stir in the butter, Parmesan, and pepper until fully incorporated.

5. Divide evenly between two serving plates and garnish with parsley.

8 oz (220g) **small ridged shell pasta** (conchiglie rigate)

2 tbsp **olive oil**

1 **shallot,** finely diced

1 clove **garlic,** finely minced

7 oz (200g) **canned white beans,** rinsed and drained

½ cup **water** (4.2oz / 120g), divided

¾ tsp **salt**

¼ tsp **MSG**

¼ cup **white wine** or champagne

1 tbsp cold **butter** (0.5oz / 15g)

¾ cup grated **Parmesan cheese** (2.6oz / 75g)

1 tsp freshly cracked **black pepper** (20 cracks), or to taste

2 tbsp chopped **fresh parsley,** to garnish

TOMATO FRIED EGGS

SERVES
2

PREP TIME
10 minutes

COOK TIME
10 minutes

When I moved to China, I was shocked at how common this dish is. But it makes so much sense. While most of the world enjoys tomato and egg variations for breakfast, in China they're turned into a saucy stir-fry and served as a side dish or over rice or noodles for lunch. This recipe is optimized for good-all-year canned tomatoes and takes less than 20 minutes to make.

DIRECTIONS

1. Remove the whole tomatoes from the can (reserve the liquid) and roughly chop into bite-sized pieces. Set aside.

2. In a small bowl, whisk together the reserved tomato liquid, cornstarch, soy sauce, ketchup, and ¼ teaspoon salt to create a slurry.

3. In a wok over medium-high heat, warm the oil until it begins to ripple. Add the ginger slices and stir-fry for 30 to 60 seconds or until fragrant.

4. Discard ginger pieces and add the scallion whites. Stir-fry for 20 to 30 seconds or until fragrant.

5. Add the eggs and slowly scramble for 2 minutes until large, soft curds form. Do not overmix, and move to the next step as soon as you see the eggs start developing a golden crust.

6. Add the chili flakes and five spice powder, and stir-fry until fragrant. Add the chopped tomato and stir-fry for 2 minutes.

7. Stir in the tomato and cornstarch slurry, and cook for 1 minute or until the sauce has thickened. Remove from the heat and add the scallion greens. Mix to combine. Garnish with cilantro and serve over rice, if desired.

1 14oz (400g) can **whole tomatoes**

1 tsp **cornstarch**

½ tbsp **light soy sauce**

1 tbsp **ketchup**

¼ tsp **salt**

2 tbsp **neutral cooking oil**

1-inch (2.5cm) piece **fresh ginger,** thickly sliced

3 **scallions,** sliced on the bias, light and dark green parts divided

3 large **eggs,** whisked

1 tsp **red chili flakes**

⅛ tsp **five spice powder**

Chopped **fresh cilantro** (optional), to garnish

Steamed **white rice** (optional), to serve

Salads

In today's oversaturated food landscape, the word "salad" does not exactly spark excitement among many foodies (unless they're currently trying to offset their sinful culinary adventures). But who said a salad has to be a soggy pile of lettuce? The world of food knows no hard rules, and there are more than enough delicious recipes around the globe that are ready to redeem salad's reputation.

Tea Leaf Coleslaw **152**

Avocado & Tomato Salad **153**

Uzbek Eggplant Salad **155**

German Potato Salad **157**

Russian Vinegret **159**

Causa **163**

Fattoush **165**

Three-Sliver Salad **168**

Tangy Spinach & Peanut Salad **169**

Sichuan-Style Wood Ear Mushrooms **171**

Salad: it Doesn't Have to Be Boring

With all due respect to leafy side salads, this category of food can be so much more! In this chapter, we're exploring different ways to dress salad and adding substance with heftier ingredients. Your definition of salad might be about to change for good.

ALL EYES EAST

If you have come this far in this book, you will already know that my years in China have deeply influenced my eating and cooking habits. While the concept of a Western-style salad might appear quite foreign to many Chinese eaters (we can start with the fact that with a few exceptions, raw vegetables are very hard to come by in Chinese food), you better believe there is an equivalent: enter *liang cai,* or **Chinese cold dishes.** If you ever thought salad was boring, try one of my suggested recipes and I'll ask you again. I'm also looking forward to having a conversation about whether these are salads or not. (They totally are.)

But as much as I love liang cai, there is one school of Asian salad making that beats them in my world. You might be expecting me to come at you with a few Thai or Vietnamese dishes, many of which could be seen as salads, but that's not it. Instead, let's look to Myanmar. I was fortunate enough to have visited and immediately found myself wondering why this Southeast Asian country was so criminally under-represented on the global food stage. The country itself is located between China, Thailand, and India, and its cuisine reflects that very well. You can find rich curries, soupy noodle dishes, and very importantly, a whole category of light sides called *thoke*. Thoke are often made up of freshly tossed veggies and greens dressed in a flavorful sauce, so you already know what they remind me of. Since I vowed to take every chance to spread the word on this amazing country's food culture, here it comes: **Burmese salads.** The first is an unexpected take on coleslaw; the second a Southeast Asian take on avocado salad.

BREAD: A SALAD'S BEST FRIEND

Of course, that is just the beginning of our salad journey. Next let me take you to the Middle East. This region is known for succulent grilled kebabs (and rightfully so), but don't forget that those kebabs usually come with a sidekick—delicious bread. And where there is bread, there is stale bread. Throwing it out would be unforgivable—stale bread upcycles quite well in the kitchen. You could, for example, cut it up and make croutons, which make so many dishes better (not just salads!). Or you go the Middle Eastern route and take croutons to a whole new level with **fattoush**. Toasted or fried old bread is not just an ingredient in this salad: it's the star of the show.

And since we're in the region, let's take a quick detour to Uzbekistan, where Levantine, Russian, and Asian techniques and flavors meet to create one of my favorite simple side salads. I don't think it has a specific name, so I just called it **Uzbek Eggplant Salad.**

THE HUMBLE POTATO

I also really wanted to include a potato salad in this book. One of the major advantages? Potato salad is great to cook in big batches to feed a lot of people, and its starchy main ingredient is quite literally a sponge that absorbs any dressing. Unlike most fresh salads, which turn soggy after merely sitting out for 15 minutes, a potato salad will only reach its peak form when rested in the fridge overnight.

We should start this mini excursion into potato salad in Germany. Germans are very, very serious about potatoes, which can sometimes be annoying, but the upshot is that I believe we have perfected the art of potato salad. There is a bit of a war going on between the mayo and the vinaigrette factions, and I'm firmly on team vinaigrette. My **German potato salad** recipe shows you how I like to make mine—it's the little additions like bits of apple that make it shine.

My family would stick to Russian potato salad recipes for the most part, though, one in particular: **vinegret.** The name might be a bit of a misnomer; in this case, it does not refer to an emulsified sour dressing but rather to a beet-and-potato salad with the addition of dill pickles or sour cabbage. With a splash of fresh sunflower seed oil right before serving, it is as classic of a *zakuska,* a Russian appetizer, as it gets.

Needless to say, potato salad was all around me growing up. When I traveled to Peru, I was delighted to discover they had a totally different but equally delicious approach to potato salad. **Causa** is a staple around the country and resembles a layered potato salad with a few distinctly Latin American influences. I should not have been surprised by the way—Peru is the home of the potato, after all, a fact easily overlooked by someone who grew up in a country that calls its own inhabitants "potatoes" sometimes.

TEA LEAF COLESLAW

SERVES

4

PREP TIME

15 minutes

COOK TIME

10 minutes + 30 minutes to chill

One of Myanmar's national dishes is *lahpet thoke* or "pickled tea leaf salad." It's the first (and so far, only) time I've had a dish that successfully uses tea leaves as an ingredient, and I think it's an idea worth exploring. Preserving your own tea leaves would probably be a bit excessive, but this quick-pickled version is your shortcut to a whole new flavor profile. Try it with this Burmese coleslaw, but don't stop there!

DIRECTIONS

1. In a large bowl, combine the cabbage, carrot, salt, and sugar. Vigorously knead with your hands for 2 minutes and set aside.

2. Steep the tea leaves in 2 cups near-boiling water for 4 minutes. Reserve the tea leaves and set aside. (Drink or discard the tea.)

3. In a small nonstick pan, heat the oil over medium-low heat. Add the shallot, garlic, and ginger. Cook for 4 minutes or until the aromatics are fragrant and lightly browned.

4. To a small food processor, add the tea leaves, lime juice, fish sauce, and the fried aromatics with their oil. Process for 1 minute or until the dressing is smooth.

5. Add the dressing to the bowl with the cabbage and carrots, along with the cilantro, peanuts, mung bean shoots, and red chili (if using). Mix until well combined. Refrigerate for at least 30 minutes before serving. Serve chilled.

¼ small head **green cabbage,** shredded

1 large **carrot,** grated

1 tsp **salt**

1½ tbsp **granulated sugar**

1 tbsp **organic sencha** or **dragon well green tea leaves** (Longjing tea)

3 tbsp **neutral cooking oil**

1 **shallot,** finely minced

1 clove **garlic,** finely minced

1-inch (2.5cm) piece **fresh ginger,** finely minced

Juice of 2 **limes**

1 tbsp **fish sauce**

¼ cup chopped **fresh cilantro,** packed

¼ cup **roasted peanuts,** crushed

1 cup **mung bean shoots**

1 **fresh Thai red chili** (optional), thinly sliced

AVOCADO & TOMATO SALAD

SERVES
2

PREP TIME
10 minutes

COOK TIME
10 minutes + 20 minutes to chill

This simple salad might only take a few minutes to whip up, but I was so happy to find a delicious avocado recipe that was not guacamole that I simply had to include it. It tastes even better when chilled before serving!

DIRECTIONS

1. To a small nonstick pan over medium-low heat, add the oil, shallot, garlic, ginger, and chili flakes. Gently simmer for 4 minutes or until fragrant and lightly browned. Remove from the heat and let cool for 3 to 5 minutes.

2. In a large bowl, combine the tomatoes, avocado, oil and aromatics, fish sauce, lime juice, sugar, salt, MSG, cilantro, and sesame seeds. Mix until well combined. Refrigerate for 20 minutes or up to 2 hours before serving.

3 tbsp **neutral cooking oil**

1 **shallot,** finely minced

1 clove **garlic,** finely minced

1-inch (2.5cm) piece **fresh ginger,** finely minced

1 tsp **red chili flakes**

2 medium **tomatoes,** diced

1 large **avocado,** diced

½ tbsp **fish sauce**

Juice of ½ **lime**

½ tsp **granulated sugar**

⅛ tsp **salt**

⅛ tsp **MSG**

¼ cup chopped **fresh cilantro,** packed

1 tbsp **sesame seeds,** toasted

UZBEK EGGPLANT SALAD

SERVES

2

PREP TIME

15 minutes + 30 minutes to cool

COOK TIME

50 minutes

Even the biggest eggplant fans will get tired of baba ganoush one day. This is exactly when it's time to whip up this simple eggplant salad, which I first had in Uzbekistan. With its tangy and garlicky flavors, it's a perfect counterpoint for hearty dishes like grilled meats.

DIRECTIONS

1. Preheat the oven to 400°F (200°C). Line a baking sheet with foil. Pierce the eggplants three times on both sides with a fork. Place on the prepared baking sheet and roast for 50 to 60 minutes or until fork-tender and charred on the outside. Place the eggplants in a sealed airtight container or plastic bag for 30 minutes to cool. (They will continue to steam as they cool, and the flesh will loosen from the skin.)

2. When safe to handle comfortably, slice lengthwise and scoop the flesh into a medium bowl. Add 2 tablespoons oil, juice of ½ lemon, garlic, cumin, and ¼ teaspoon salt. Mash and stir with a fork until well combined. Spread evenly over a serving plate.

3. In a medium bowl, combine the tomato, cucumber, carrot, bell pepper, remaining 1 tablespoon oil, dill, cilantro, brown sugar, remaining 1 teaspoon salt, and juice of the remaining ½ lemon. (See note.)

4. Spread the mixed vegetables over the eggplant paste. Season with freshly cracked pepper to taste and garnish with toasted sunflower seeds, if desired.

NOTE: For a more composed and aesthetically pleasing salad, dress the vegetables separately before spreading them on the eggplant.

2 medium **eggplants** (about 25oz / 700g in total)

3 tbsp **cold-pressed sunflower seed oil, walnut oil,** or **neutral cooking oil,** divided

Juice of 1 **lemon,** divided

1 clove **garlic,** grated

¼ tsp **ground cumin**

1¼ tsp **salt,** divided

1 medium **tomato,** deseeded and julienned

⅓ **cucumber,** deseeded and julienned

1 **carrot,** julienned

½ **green bell pepper,** deseeded and julienned

3 tbsp chopped **fresh dill**

3 tbsp chopped **fresh cilantro**

½ tsp **brown sugar**

Freshly cracked **black pepper** (optional), to serve

2 tbsp **toasted sunflower seeds** (optional), to serve

GERMAN POTATO SALAD

SERVES
6

PREP TIME
20 minutes

COOK TIME
20 minutes + 4 hours to chill

In Germany, there is a fierce battle over the right way to dress potato salad. In some regions, mayo is the base of choice, but Berlin is firmly on team vinaigrette. Make this salad next time you have a lot of people over or need to bring a guaranteed crowd-pleaser to a potluck!

DIRECTIONS

1. Place the potatoes in a large pot and cover with salted water. Bring to a boil and then cook over medium-high heat for 15 minutes or until fork-tender. Drain the potatoes, and cool for 15 minutes. When cool, cut into ½-inch (1.25cm) cubes.

2. To make the dressing, in a small container (with a lid), combine all ingredients. Secure the lid and shake vigorously until combined.

3. In a large bowl, combine the potatoes, onion, apple, cucumber, pickles, chives, dill, and dressing. Gently mix until well combined. Cover and refrigerate for at least 4 hours or—even better—overnight. Traditionally served cold.

2¼ lb (1kg) unpeeled **waxy potatoes,** well scrubbed

1 medium **red onion,** diced

1 unpeeled **red apple** (4.9oz / 140g), diced

½ **cucumber** (6oz / 170g), diced

3½ oz (100g) diced **sweet gherkins** or **bread and butter pickles**

2 tbsp finely chopped **fresh chives**

2 tbsp finely chopped **fresh dill**

FOR THE DRESSING

¼ cup **sunflower oil** or **olive oil** (1.9oz / 55g)

3 tbsp **Dijon mustard** (0.9oz / 25g)

½ cup **pickle juice** (4fl oz / 125ml)

2 tbsp **white vinegar**

1½ tbsp **granulated sugar**

¾ tsp **salt**

1 tsp freshly cracked **black pepper** (20 cracks)

RUSSIAN VINEGRET
(BEET SALAD)

SERVES	5-6
PREP TIME	10 minutes
COOK TIME	25 minutes + 30 minutes to chill

If you open my family's fridge, there's a 99 percent chance you'll find a bowl of Russian *vinegret* somewhere. This simple, earthy salad is a fantastic side dish and goes surprisingly well with most European food. It will also invoke some serious nostalgia in anyone with a babushka (or two).

DIRECTIONS

1. Place the whole, unpeeled potatoes and carrots in a medium pot. Add cold water to cover the vegetables by at least 2 inches (5cm) and 1 teaspoon salt. Bring to a boil over high heat. When boiling, reduce heat to medium and cook for 15 to 20 minutes or until the vegetables are fork-tender. Remove the vegetables from the pot, let cool, and peel with a butter knife. Dice and transfer to a large bowl.

2. To the same bowl, add the beets, peas, sauerkraut, scallion, shallot, oil, remaining ¼ teaspoon salt, and pepper to taste. Mix until well combined. Cover with plastic wrap and refrigerate for at least 30 minutes or up to 2 days before serving.

NOTES: Wear food-safe rubber gloves to prevent staining your hands when handling beets. While untraditional, using pickled beets instead of precooked can add a piquant flavor.

Frozen peas are generally a better choice for most applications and would work as a substitute in this recipe. Just be aware that you would not find a single babushka making it this way; without canned peas, it's just not old-school vinaigrette.

You can replace all or part of the sauerkraut with diced dill pickles.

2 large **waxy potatoes** (10.6oz / 300g)

2 **carrots** (4.6oz / 130g)

1¼ tsp **salt**, divided

3-4 precooked **red beets** (10.6oz / 300g), diced (see note)

3½ oz (100g) **canned peas**, drained (see note)

6 oz (170g) **Russian Sauerkraut** (page 227) or **store-bought sauerkraut**, chopped (see note)

1 **scallion**, chopped

1 **shallot**, diced

⅓ cup **sunflower oil**

Freshly cracked **black pepper**, to taste

The Enigma of the Salad

As I was preparing to research dishes for this chapter, I wanted to come up with a working definition of what a salad actually is. Sounds easy enough, doesn't it? Turns out I have no idea what salad is supposed to be. Let me explain.

I thought salad was made from raw ingredients. But that doesn't check out. We have pasta salads, potato salads, meat salads . . . the list goes on.

I thought salad was always served cold—nope. In addition to winter salads made with roasted veggies, there are plenty of dishes like steak salad where at least some of the ingredients are cooked and served above room temperature.

I thought salad was always a side dish. But then I remembered Caesar salad, which is really just a way to eat a chicken and cheese sandwich from a bowl.

I thought salad was always tossed in a bowl, but there is a whole category of composed salads like caprese, where ingredients are presented in a particular way.

I thought salad was savory, but I have had fruit salads countless times. (Let's not even mention JELL-O salads, cookie salads, and the like.)

So, what is a salad? I guess you just know it when you see it.

CAUSA
(PERUVIAN LAYERED POTATO SALAD)

SERVES
6

PREP TIME
50 minutes

COOK TIME
45 minutes + 1 hour to chill

Growing up in Germany, I was certain I knew of every way to eat potatoes. But Peru might be on a whole other level. It is, after all, where the potato was first cultivated. Causa is Peru's unique version of a layered potato salad. You'll find it in humble cantinas across the country, but bougie versions of this dish are no rarity in fine dining establishments either.

DIRECTIONS

1. Fill a medium saucepan with lightly salted water and bring to a simmer over medium-high heat. Add the chicken breast and simmer for 15 minutes. Remove from the pot and shred. Set aside.

2. Place the potatoes in a medium pot and add cold water to cover. Bring to a boil over medium-high heat and cook for 30 minutes or until fork-tender. Drain and transfer to a large bowl.

3. To the potatoes, add 5 tablespoons lime juice along with the butter, paprika, and 1½ teaspoons salt. Mash until a few small chunks remain, just shy of being completely smooth. Set aside.

4. In another large bowl, combine the shredded chicken, eggs, olives, tomato, shallot, mayonnaise, and ½ teaspoon salt. Mix everything together with a fork, smashing the eggs into small chunks. Set aside.

5. Scoop the avocado flesh into a medium bowl and mash with the remaining ½ tablespoon lime juice and remaining ¼ teaspoon salt.

6. In an 8 x 8-inch (20 x 20cm) baking dish, begin to layer the different components. Start by spreading about two-thirds of the mashed potato mixture over the bottom of the dish. On top of that, spread the avocado mixture, then the chicken-and-egg mixture. Top it off with the remaining mashed potatoes.

7. Smooth the surface with slightly damp hands. Cover tightly with plastic wrap and refrigerate for at least 1 hour or (even better) overnight.

8. Before serving, spread a thin layer of mayonnaise over the potatoes. Sprinkle with cilantro and grated Parmesan. Slice into pieces (like a lasagna) and serve chilled but not cold.

12 oz (350g) **chicken breast**

3 lb (1.4kg) medium **potatoes,** peeled and halved

5½ tbsp **lime juice** (2.3oz / 65g), divided

2 tbsp **butter,** melted

½ tbsp **mild paprika**

2¼ tsp **salt,** divided

3 hard-boiled **eggs**

¼ cup finely chopped **black olives** (2.1oz / 60g)

1 medium **tomato,** finely diced

1 large **shallot,** finely diced

½ cup **mayonnaise** (3.5oz / 100g)

2 **avocados**

FOR THE TOPPING

2 tbsp **mayonnaise** (1.2oz / 35g)

3 sprigs **fresh cilantro,** leaves only, chopped

1½ tbsp grated **Parmesan cheese** (0.7oz / 20g)

FATTOUSH
(LEBANESE-STYLE BREAD SALAD)

SERVES	2
PREP TIME	10 minutes
COOK TIME	15 minutes

The name of this dish translates from Arabic to "breadcrumbs," which is a hint to the hero ingredient: bread. While you could use the freshly baked kind, this recipe is really a genius way to use up stale white bread. Italians know a similar salad as *panzanella,* so for this recipe, I borrowed a few techniques from them as well.

DIRECTIONS

1. Preheat the oven to 350°F (180°C). Line a baking sheet with parchment paper.

2. In a large bowl, toss the bread cubes in olive oil. Spread evenly on the prepared baking sheet and bake for 15 minutes or until golden brown. Turn halfway through baking.

3. In the same large bowl, toss the cucumber, tomatoes, and radishes with the salt. Set aside.

4. After removing the bread cubes from the oven, drain the accumulated liquid from the salted vegetables into a small bowl. To that, add the lemon juice, tahini, and za'atar (if using). Mix to combine. (The tahini might cause the mixture to thicken; this is normal.)

5. Return the dressing to the bowl with the veggies. Add the lettuce, olives, mint, parsley, Thai basil (if using), and toasted bread. Toss to combine.

NOTE: Any leavened and fluffy but ideally stale white bread will work. I've had success with fluffy pitas (not the super thin ones), ciabatta, baguette, and even sourdough.

5oz (150g) **stale white bread,** cubed (see note)

1 tbsp **olive oil**

¾ cup diced **cucumber** (5.3oz / 150g)

⅔ cup diced **tomatoes** (5.3oz / 150g)

⅓ cup halved **radishes** (2.8oz / 80g)

½ tsp **salt**

Juice of ¼ **lemon**

2 tbsp **tahini**

1 tsp **za'atar** (optional)

¼ head **romaine lettuce** (3.5 oz / 100g), chopped

2½ oz (80g) **mixed olives,** pitted

4 sprigs **fresh mint,** leaves only

4 sprigs **fresh parsley,** leaves only

4 sprigs **fresh Thai basil,** leaves only (optional)

THREE-SLIVER SALAD
(CHINESE TOFU, CELERY & CARROT SALAD)

SERVES
3-4

PREP TIME
20 minutes

COOK TIME
15 minutes

The "three slivers" this Chinese salad is named after are not fixed ingredients, but it's a common concept. Most of the time, the formula breaks down to something green, something red, and something tofu. No matter which set of ingredients you end up going for, if you're looking for a quick, savory side dish that packs a punch, this is it!

DIRECTIONS

1. Rehydrate the dried tofu skins for 20 minutes in hot water; drain. Without unrolling them, slice the tofu skins into thin ribbons and unfurl.

2. In a saucepan with boiling water, blanch the tofu skins, celery, and carrot for 1 minute. Strain and chill under running cold water for 30 seconds. Set aside.

3. In a small heatproof bowl, mix the chili flakes, garlic, scallions, Sichuan pepper, salt, and sugar.

4. In a small pan, heat the oil until light wisps of smoke appear. Pour the hot oil over the spice mix. Infuse for 2 minutes. Stir in the soy sauce, vinegar, MSG, and sesame oil.

5. In a large bowl, combine the blanched vegetables, sauce, and cilantro stalks.

6. Serve at room temperature or lightly chilled as a side dish. Always give the salad a fresh mix right before transferring to a serving plate and eating.

10 rolls **dried tofu skin**

2 stalks **celery,** julienned

1 **carrot,** julienned

1 tbsp **red chili flakes**

1 tbsp minced **garlic**

1 tbsp minced **scallions**

½ tsp **ground Sichuan pepper**

1 tsp **salt**

½ tsp **granulated sugar**

2 tbsp **neutral cooking oil**

1 tbsp **soy sauce**

2 tsp **dark Chinese vinegar**

¼ tsp **MSG**

1 tsp **toasted sesame oil**

½ cup **cilantro stalks,** cut into 2-inch (4cm) segments

TANGY SPINACH & PEANUT SALAD

SERVES
2-3

PREP TIME
5 minutes

COOK TIME
10 minutes

This is hands down my favorite way to eat spinach. The short blanching time preserves some of its original bite, while peanuts and sesame oil perfectly highlight the nutty flavor. Popeye would be proud!

DIRECTIONS

1. Fill a large stockpot halfway with water and bring to a boil over high heat. Add the spinach and cook for 2 minutes until wilted. Drain and transfer to an ice water bath to stop the cooking. Drain again and squeeze as much moisture out of the spinach between your hands as you can.

2. Place the spinach in a large bowl and loosen if needed after squeezing. Add the peanuts, vinegar, sugar, soy sauce, MSG, sesame oil, garlic, and salt. Mix well to combine.

3. Transfer to a serving dish, and top with additional peanuts and sliced red chili peppers, if desired. Serve immediately.

2lb (1kg) **bunch spinach,** trimmed and washed

½ cup **roasted peanuts** (2.1oz / 60g), crushed

2 tbsp **dark Chinese vinegar**

2 tsp **granulated sugar**

1 tbsp **soy sauce**

¼ tsp **MSG**

1 tsp **toasted sesame oil**

1 tbsp minced **garlic**

½ tsp **salt**

1 small **red chili** (optional), thinly sliced

SICHUAN-STYLE
WOOD EAR MUSHROOMS

SERVES
2-3

PREP TIME
5 minutes + 2 hours inactive time

COOK TIME
1 minute

You may have noticed from the selection of recipes in this book that I am not a fan of mushrooms. I just don't enjoy their usually mushy texture. But wood ear mushrooms are a rare exception. They have an almost crunchy texture, which is highlighted in this refreshing cold dish.

DIRECTIONS

1. Rehydrate the mushrooms by soaking them in room temperature water for 1 hour. Using your hands, remove the tough center of the mushroom by pulling off the parts around it and tearing them into bite-sized pieces.

2. In a small saucepan of boiling water, blanch the mushrooms for 1 minute; drain.

3. In a large bowl, combine the blanched mushrooms, chili flakes, Sichuan pepper, soy sauce, MSG, vinegar, sugar, sesame oil, ginger, and both varieties of sliced chilies. Mix thoroughly.

4. Cover and refrigerate for 1 hour, stirring every 15 minutes. Mix well before serving, and garnish with scallions and cilantro. Serve cold.

½ oz (15g) dried **black wood ear mushrooms** (also called mu-erh mushrooms)

2 tsp **red chili flakes**

½ tsp ground **green Sichuan pepper**

2 tbsp **soy sauce**

¼ tsp **MSG**

1 tbsp **dark Chinese vinegar**

1 tsp **granulated sugar**

1 tsp **sesame oil**

1 tsp minced **fresh ginger**

2 **fresh Thai red chilies,** thinly sliced

1 small **yellow chili,** thinly sliced

1 **scallion,** thinly sliced, to garnish

¼ cup chopped **fresh cilantro,** to garnish

Dinner

It's probably safe to say dinner is the most versatile meal of the day. It can be a quick affair of convenience, but it can also stretch for hours and turn into one of those epic nights where the food and good times just don't seem to end. No matter which one you go for, I believe this chapter holds a few good ideas for you!

Hainanese Chicken Rice **178**

Beef Burgundy **181**

Hot Pot **182**

Sichuan-Style Hot Pot Broth Base **182**

Clear Hot Pot Broth Base **184**

Hot Pot Add-Ins **184**

Hot Pot Dipping Sauce **185**

Chicken Adobo **187**

Easy Plov **191**

Gu Lou Yuk **193**

Lomo Saltado **195**

Peking Duck Chicken Wraps **197**

Dinner: the Grand Finale

Invite some friends, throw together a playlist, and stock up on cold drinks, because no matter which one of these recipes you go for, your next dinner party will be unforgettable.

WINNER WINNER CHICKEN DINNER

I'm not exactly sure why, but there was a point in my life when I realized chicken and rice is the perfect meal. Just like every culture has its dumpling, I suspect most cultures also have their versions of chicken and rice. Even though I happened to have picked a few Asian-inspired recipes, there are many other examples across every single continent.

My all-time favorite is, and always will be, **Hainanese chicken rice.** Not just because of how delicious it is, although that would be reason enough. I'm also eternally connected to this dish through one of my earliest and most profound food culture lessons (which you can read about later in this chapter).

Another inspiration comes from the Philippines, where **chicken adobo** is on nearly every person's list of favorite dishes. Despite its name, this adobo has almost nothing to do with its Mexican namesake—but it is a reminder of the countries' shared colonial past.

The third place that has a chicken rice dish near and dear to my heart is Hong Kong (technically, also an island). **Gu lou yuk,** also known as sweet-and-sour pork, is not just a classic in all of Cantonese cuisine but also one of the dishes that has helped Chinese cuisine enter the mainstream in Western eating cultures.

You may have noticed the "pork" part of this chicken dish—let me explain. Traditionally, slivers of pork are deep-fried for this dish, then brought together in a delicious sauce before serving over rice. When a popular fast-food chain ran a promotion once selling chicken nuggets, savvy Hong Kong moms filled their freezers to the brim, and what followed was a few months of kids eating all sorts of improvised dishes from upcycled nuggets. The genius part is that this eliminated the most laborious step in making gu lou yuk, turning it into a 20-minute recipe. A secret I did not want to keep from you!

GETTING SERIOUS

Speaking of chicken—while my love for Peking duck runs deep, I will accept that it is out of reach for the average (or even the advanced) home cook. But what is not out of reach is my **Peking duck chicken wrap,** which I hope will bring some of the flavors you love in Peking duck to the home kitchen in a fraction of the time.

Another favorite food memory of mine is eating plov in Uzbekistan, a country that travelers should pay more attention to. Due to the country's geography, its food landscape is not very diverse, but the dishes commonly found in the country have been perfected by this unique nation. Without having to think twice, Uzbekistan's national dish would have to be **plov**—the granddaddy of rice pilaf. They have even developed special varieties of rice specifically for plov, which are not easily sourced outside of Uzbekistan because there are strict export limitations. I consider myself lucky to have been permitted to bring home one kilogram for personal consumption. Don't worry, my simplified version of plov gets by without it and will be on the table in under 30 minutes!

I would also like to address the elephant in the room: for all the food in this book, where are the French classics? It might be my tendency to go against the flow, but this entire category seemed so overrepresented yet disconnected from contemporary global food culture to me that I never developed an interest in it. On a trip to Paris, I did eventually bring myself to explore it a bit, and I have to admit, it might not be novel, but I can see why French cuisine has dominated restaurant culture for a long time. The **beef Burgundy** recipe you will find in this chapter is more than a mere token—it's your ticket to a luxurious yet comforting French dinner. Pro tip: get two bottles of wine because you will need an entire one for this dish!

And since we're talking beef, let's take a look at **lomo saltado,** a dish widely consumed in Peru and its neighboring countries. Nobody would dispute its origin as Latin American, but it's also a testament to the influence of Chinese cuisine in the region. For historical reasons, Chinese migration to the Pacific coast of South America began in the nineteenth century and never really stopped. And that, kids, is why a local food staple is a wok stir-fry seasoned with soy sauce and ginger.

ALL IN

Finally, for the most social food adventurers, I recommend hosting a **hot pot** party. If you are looking for that epic hours-long dinner experience, there is simply no better way. Other than making a hot pot soup base, this is also barely a recipe and more of a lifestyle: you get near total freedom to choose what you want to offer as hot pot add-ins! The only thing more fun than this is mixing your own dipping sauce. I never waste this opportunity to eat way more garlic in one sitting than I'd dare recommending to anyone around me!

HAINANESE CHICKEN RICE

SERVES
2-4

PREP TIME
20 minutes

COOK TIME
90 minutes

1 whole **free-range chicken** (about 3lb / 1.5kg), ideally corn fed

4 thick slices **fresh ginger,** smashed

3 **scallions,** tied into knots

1 tbsp **salt**

1 tbsp **granulated sugar**

1 tsp **MSG**

1 tbsp **toasted sesame oil**

FOR THE RICE

2 cups **jasmine rice**

3 tbsp **coconut oil** or **neutral cooking oil**

1 tbsp minced **fresh ginger**

3 cloves **garlic,** minced

2 **shallots,** minced

TO SERVE

Cucumbers, peeled and cut into batons

It's safe to say I have made no other dish as many times as Hainanese chicken rice. If you can get your hands on a very high-quality bird, this is without a doubt the best way to appreciate it. On a similar note, beware that making it with an ordinary chicken might be disappointing. No matter what you go for, don't forget that the real hero of this dish is the rice, not the chicken. There are countless variants and different methods of making Hainanese chicken rice, but this is my collection of traditional as well as outside-the-box tips!

DIRECTIONS

1. To prepare the chicken, stand the whole chicken over a bottle or large can in the sink and slowly pour boiling water over it, scalding it on all sides. Make sure to get every piece of skin. (This step is important for the final texture of the chicken skin.)

2. Taking care not to tear the skin, transfer the chicken to a work surface. Stuff the sliced ginger and scallion knots inside the cavity of the chicken and transfer to a large stockpot.

3. Add enough cold water to submerge the chicken. Add the salt, sugar, and MSG, and bring to a simmer over medium-high heat. Reduce the heat to low, cover with a lid, and simmer for 20 minutes. (The chicken should remain fully submerged in the liquid while simmering.) Remove the pot from the heat and let sit, still covered, for 15 minutes, allowing the residual heat to finish cooking the chicken.

4. Meanwhile, rinse the rice thoroughly and let it soak in a bowl of water for 20 minutes. Drain and discard the water, and set the rice aside.

5. When done cooking, carefully transfer the chicken into an ice water bath and set aside. Reserve the stock.

6. To make the rice, to a large skillet over medium heat, add the oil, ginger, garlic, and shallots. Sauté for 3 to 5 minutes or until the aromatics just begin to caramelize. Add the washed rice. Stir-fry to toast the rice for another 3 to 5 minutes.

7. Transfer the rice mixture to a rice cooker and cook according to rice cooker instructions using the reserved chicken stock instead of water. (Alternatively, if you do not have a rice cooker, transfer to a medium saucepan. Cook the rice as instructed on the package, using the reserved chicken stock instead of water.)

GINGER SCALLION OIL

1 tbsp grated **fresh ginger**

1 clove **garlic,** minced

1 **scallion,** minced

½ tbsp **granulated sugar**

¼ tsp **salt**

3 tbsp **neutral cooking oil**

1 tbsp **soy sauce**

½ tsp **toasted sesame oil**

ZESTY SRIRACHA DIP

¼ cup **sriracha**

1 tbsp **granulated sugar**

1 tbsp **lime juice**

¼ tsp **MSG**

8. Meanwhile, prepare the dips. **For the Ginger Scallion Oil,** combine the ginger, garlic, scallion, sugar, and salt in a small heat proof mixing bowl. In a small saucepan, heat the cooking oil until wisps of smoke appear. Carefully pour the hot oil evenly over the ingredients in the mixing bowl. Infuse for 30 seconds. Stir in the soy sauce and sesame oil. **For the Zesty Sriracha Dip,** in a small bowl, mix all ingredients until homogenous. As an optional third dip, make **Kuya Rafa's Sawsawan Dip** (page 215) or use a simple 1:1 mix of light soy sauce and Chinese dark vinegar.

9. Remove the chicken from the ice bath and carefully pat it dry. Brush with sesame oil. Carve and debone the chicken and cut into bite-sized pieces, keeping the skin over each individual piece of chicken intact, if possible. Alternatively, carve off the chicken breasts and tear the rest of the meat off the bones and carcass, then chop into bite-sized pieces for a more rustic but much easier method.

10. Transfer the chicken to a platter, add the cucumber, and serve with individual bowls of rice and dipping sauces on the side.

BEEF BURGUNDY

SERVES
3-6
PREP TIME
15 minutes
COOK TIME
4 hours

Believe it or not, I had been running my cooking channel for years before I cooked my first French dish. Once I realized this oversight, I ate my way through Paris and settled on *bœuf bourguignon* (beef Burgundy) as my introduction to French cooking. The ultra-rich flavor and luxurious texture of this classic beef stew will bring you back to life even on the gloomiest of days.

DIRECTIONS

1. To a large heavy pot over medium-high heat, add 2 tablespoons olive oil and the bacon. Cook until the fat has rendered, 3 to 5 minutes. Transfer the bacon bits to a plate and set aside, leaving the rendered fat in the pot.

2. Add the stew meat and sear the outside, 1 to 2 minutes on each side. Remove and set aside. (There should be some residual fat left in the pot.)

3. To the same pot, add the white onion and cook for 2 to 3 minutes before adding the garlic and carrots. Sauté for 2 to 4 minutes. Return the beef and bacon to the pot. Add the parsley, 3 sprigs of thyme, and the bay leaves. Pour in the whole bottle of red wine. The liquid should cover the meat; if you do not have enough, add water to cover. Add ½ teaspoon salt and 2 teaspoons pepper. Cover, and simmer for at least 2 hours or (even better) up to 4 hours. Add more water as needed to ensure that the meat remains submerged.

4. Meanwhile, in a medium skillet over medium-low heat, melt the butter with the remaining 2 tablespoons olive oil. Add the mushrooms, halved pearl onions, and remaining 2 sprigs of thyme. Season with salt and pepper, and cook, stirring occasionally, for about 5 minutes or until the onions are browned. Remove the thyme stems. Set the mushrooms and onions aside.

5. Place a steamer over a large saucepan or pot filled with boiling water. Steam the potatoes for 25 minutes or until fork-tender. Set aside.

6. Once the stew has cooked and the beef is tender, remove and set aside the beef, bacon, and carrots. Strain the broth through a mesh sieve, and then return it to the pot. Discard the thyme stems, parsley stalks, and bay leaves. Return the pot to the stove top over medium-high heat.

7. In a small bowl, whisk the cornstarch in water until dissolved to create a slurry. Add the slurry to the broth. Simmer for 15 minutes or until the sauce is silky and coats the back of a spoon. Taste and season with salt if needed.

8. To finish, stir in the garlic, butter, thyme, parsley, and MSG. Add the potatoes, mushrooms, and onion. Return the carrots, beef, and bacon. Cook, stirring frequently, until everything is hot and coated in the sauce, about 5 minutes.

4 tbsp **extra virgin olive oil**, divided

5 oz (150g) **bacon**, diced

1½ lb (700g) **beef stew meat** (preferably chuck), cut into chunks

1 large **white onion**, diced

2 cloves **garlic**, crushed

2 medium **carrots**, cut into large chunks

2 sprigs **fresh parsley**

5 sprigs **fresh thyme**, divided

2 **bay leaves**

1 (750ml) bottle **Burgundy red wine** (or any Pinot Noir)

½ tsp **salt**, plus more to taste

2 tsp freshly cracked **black pepper** (20 cracks), plus more to taste

1 tbsp **butter**

7-8 **button mushrooms**, halved

3-4 **pearl onions** or very small onions, halved

1 lb (500g) small **waxy potatoes**

1 tbsp **cornstarch**

¼ cup **water**

FOR FINISHING

1 small clove **garlic**, minced

1 tbsp **butter**

2 sprigs **fresh thyme**, leaves only

2 tbsp finely chopped **fresh parsley**

¼ tsp **MSG**

SICHUAN-STYLE
HOT POT BASE BROTH

MAKES
7 cups

PREP TIME
10 minutes

COOK TIME
15 minutes

Ever had an epic five-hour dinner? If yes, it was probably hot pot; and if not, you should really try hot pot! All you need to do is put a portable hot plate in the center of a dining table, fill it with one of the hot pot base broths (or both, if you are the lucky owner of a yin-and-yang-style split pot), spread any add-ins your heart desires around it, and go to town with your friends. For the uninitiated: pick any raw ingredients you like, drop them in the hot broth and fish them out as they're done cooking. Then dip them into a bowl of hot pot sauce, and enjoy. Pro tip: slotted spoons are your friend! And be sure to refill the pot with water when too much of the broth has evaporated.

DIRECTIONS

1. In a large, shallow saucepan over medium heat, heat the beef tallow, bay leaves, cinnamon stick, star anise, fennel, licorice root, cardamom, cumin, and cloves. Cook for 3 to 5 minutes, stirring occasionally, until the spices are fragrant and the ingredients begin to brown.

2. Add the ginger, leek, garlic, fermented black bean paste, fermented chili and bean paste, Sichuan peppercorns, and chili flakes. Stirring occasionally, sauté for 2 minutes.

3. Add the water—it should be enough to reach a depth of about 3 inches (7.5cm)—followed by the soy sauce, baijiu, sugar, and salt. Adjust salt level to taste. Simmer, covered, for at least 10 minutes. Strain the broth and discard the solids.

4. To serve, place the pan on a portable burner or hot plate at the center of the table. Keep the broth simmering over medium-low heat, and occasionally add water throughout the meal.

¾ cup **beef tallow** or **vegetable oil**

2 **bay leaves**

1 **cinnamon stick**

4 **star anise pods**

1 tbsp **fennel seeds**

1 tbsp **dried licorice root**

2 **black cardamom pods**

1 tbsp **cumin seeds**

2 whole **cloves**

10 slices **fresh ginger**

½ **leek,** white and light green part only

10 cloves **garlic,** smashed

2 tbsp **fermented black bean paste**

2 tbsp **fermented chili and bean paste** (doubanjiang)

1 tbsp whole **Sichuan peppercorns**

¼ cup **red chili flakes**

6 cups **water,** plus more for serving

2 tbsp **soy sauce**

¼ cup **baijiu** or **Chinese cooking wine**

1 tbsp **granulated sugar**

1 tsp **salt,** or to taste

CLEAR HOT POT BROTH BASE
(VEGAN)

MAKES
6 cups

PREP TIME
5 minutes

COOK TIME
15 minutes

DIRECTIONS

1. Place all ingredients a large, shallow saucepan. Add water to cover by about 3 inches (7-8cm).

2. Cover and simmer over medium-low heat for 15 minutes. Adjust salt level to taste.

3. To serve, place the pan on a hot plate at the center of the table. Keep simmering over medium-low heat, and add water as needed.

4 dried **shiitake mushrooms**

1 **leek,** light green and white part, cut into 3 segments

2 **star anise pods**

2-inch (5cm) piece **fresh ginger,** sliced

1 ear of **corn,** quartered

½ cup **soy milk**

1 tbsp **granulated sugar**

1 tbsp **cooking wine**

1 tbsp **soy sauce**

½ tbsp **MSG**

½ tbsp **salt,** or to taste

HOT POT ADD-INS

An Asian supermarket with a good selection of Chinese products is the best destination for hot pot add-ins. There you will likely find presliced hot pot meat in the freezer section, as well as a wide variety of other frozen meats, fish, and seafood. Not to mention you'll find everything from sauces to special vegetables there as well!

MEAT (RAW)
Lamb, very thinly sliced

Beef, very thinly sliced

Pork, very thinly sliced

Chicken breast, thinly sliced

Meatballs

Frog legs

Chicken hearts

Tripe

FISH AND SEAFOOD (RAW)
Shrimp, deveined

Shrimp balls

Fish balls

Squid

Squid balls

TOFU
Tofu sheets, cut into ribbons

Firm tofu

Fried tofu

Tofu puffs

Dried tofu rolls, rehydrated

STARCHY BOIS
Instant noodle

Thin wheat noodle nests

Glass noodles

Rice cakes

Sweet potato noodles

MUSHROOMS
Enoki, separated into bunches

Fresh shiitake, roughly chopped

Rehydrated wood ear mushrooms, whole or chopped

Oyster mushrooms, chopped

STURDY VEGGIES (RAW BITE-SIZED PIECES)
Potatoes

Okra

Lotus root

Asparagus

Broccoli

Cauliflower

Chinese yam

Pumpkin or squash

Corn cobs, quartered

LEAFY VEGGIES
Bok choy

Spinach

Water spinach (ong choy)

Chinese broccoli (kai lan)

Choi sam

Chrysanthemum leaves

OTHER
Leftover Youtiao (page 23), sliced

Quail eggs

Rehydrated gluten puffs

Duck blood

Dumplings

HOT POT DIPPING SAUCE

SERVES
4

PREP TIME
5 minutes

COOK TIME
5 minutes

½ cup **Chinese sesame paste** or **tahini (room temperature)**

½ cup **smooth natural peanut butter**

1 tbsp **toasted sesame oil**

½ tbsp **Chiu Chow Chili Oil** (page 205)

½ cup wam **water**

1 tbsp **soy sauce**

1 tbsp **Chinese dark vinegar**

¼ tsp **salt**, or to taste

2 cloves **garlic**, minced

2 **scallions**, finely minced

¼ cup chopped **fresh cilantro**, packed

There are absolutely no rules when it comes to hot pot dipping sauces. Usually, every person mixes their own quick sauce from a little buffet of condiments. Feel free to play around with the ingredients here or add totally new ones to your liking!

DIRECTIONS

1. In a medium bowl, combine the sesame paste, peanut butter, sesame oil, chili oil, and water. With a sturdy spoon, carefully mix to combine until smooth. (This will seem difficult in the beginning but will get easier after 2 to 3 minutes.) Stir in the soy sauce, vinegar, and salt.

2. Divide evenly among four small serving bowls. Into each bowl, add a bit of garlic, scallions, and cilantro.

CHICKEN ADOBO
WITH GARLIC RICE

My favorite chicken-and-rice dish has got to be Filipino-style chicken adobo. The sour and savory adobo flavor profile is very popular in Southeast Asia, where it is used for everything from pork to octopus. There are simpler iterations of this dish, but I've made a few unconventional adjustments—like the addition of coconut milk and citrus—for an added layer of excitement.

DIRECTIONS

1. To make the marinade, in a large bowl, whisk together all ingredients. Score the chicken drumsticks and add them to the marinade, turning to fully coat. Cover and refrigerate for at least 30 minutes or up to overnight.

2. Remove the chicken from the marinade. Reserve the marinade and pat the chicken dry. Set the marinade aside.

3. In a Dutch oven over medium-high heat, heat the oil. Add the chicken and brown on all sides. Add the water to deglaze the pan, scraping up any browned bits. Add the reserved marinade. (The chicken should be fully covered in liquid; if not, add more water as needed.)

4. Cover the Dutch oven with a lid and bring to a simmer for 40 minutes. Flip the chicken halfway through cooking.

5. Meanwhile, make the garlic rice. To a large skillet over low heat, add the oil and garlic. Gently stir-fry to infuse the oil for 5 minutes or until the garlic begins to turn golden brown. Add the rice and toast for 3 minutes, stirring occasionally. Transfer to a rice cooker, add water, and cook as instructed on the package. (Alternatively, if you do not have a rice cooker, transfer to a medium-sized saucepan. Cook the rice as instructed on the package.)

6. Remove the chicken from the sauce and set aside. Remove the bay leaves, ginger, and lemongrass. Reduce the marinade until it coats the back of a spoon. Stir in coconut milk and let it come up to a gentle simmer.

7. Plate the chicken, drizzle generously with sauce, and garnish with scallions to taste. Serve with a bowl of garlic rice.

SERVES
3-4

PREP TIME
20 minutes + 30 minutes to marinate

COOK TIME
60 minutes

---

8 **chicken drumsticks**

2 tbsp **neutral cooking oil**

½ cup **water**

⅓ cup **coconut milk**

Scallions, finely chopped, to garnish

FOR THE MARINADE

½ cup **rice vinegar** or white vinegar

¼ cup **light soy sauce**

¼ cup **dark soy sauce**

1 tbsp **granulated sugar**

Juice of 1 **tangerine**

Juice of 1 **lime**

8 cloves **garlic**, crushed and roughly chopped

4 **bay leaves**

1 tbsp whole **black peppercorns**

2 thick slices **ginger**, crushed

2 stalks **lemongrass**, crushed

FOR THE RICE

¼ cup **neutral cooking oil**

4 cloves **garlic**, minced

1½ cups **jasmine rice**, well rinsed

1½ cups **water**

The Pursuit of Hainanese Chicken Rice

Could you say which dish you have cooked more times than any other in your life? For me, that's an easy question to answer: it's Hainanese chicken rice. Hundreds of hours have gone into researching this dish for me, and dozens of chickens had to give their lives. (No worries, many people were fed in the process!) And it all started with the perhaps biggest culinary misunderstanding of my life.

The year was 2006—it seems like an eternity ago. I was barely of age and hadn't even graduated high school yet. For summer break, a friend and I signed up to volunteer as English teachers in Hainan, China's southernmost island province. We had never heard of Hainan before, but the island sounded good to us.

The small village where we ended up staying was buried deep in the tropical jungles of Hainan, a few hours away from the nearest city Wenchang. We spent our mornings teaching primary school kids to count to 10 in English and maybe to introduce themselves. I don't think they retained any of it, but it was great to hang out with kids who had never seen a non-Chinese person before and got visibly excited over it. For us, it was a fantastic opportunity to catch a glimpse of life in a country we knew absolutely nothing about back then.

How little we knew about the place and its food became apparent when one day, we were invited to a wedding by a local man we nicknamed Mr. Sanchez. We called him that because for some reason he was walking around with a big cowboy hat, a handlebar mustache, and a poncho. Mr. Sanchez did not speak English, but he was a great drinker. The day of the wedding—apparently his friend's—he came to pick us up, but he didn't come empty-handed. Many cups of clear liquor in, he sat both me and my friend on his motorbike and drove us through the dirt roads of Hainan in full darkness, laughing like a maniac with his poncho fluttering in the wind. We were terrified, but the situation was so surreal, we barely had time to question our decisions.

Eventually, we arrived at a beautiful village wedding. Burnt into my memory for all time is the wedding banquet. Giant round tables filled with plates and plates of local delicacies, each one prettier and more fragrant than the last. My friend and I immediately dug in and went for the many types of seafood on the table. When Mr. Sanchez and his friends tried to get us to taste a bland-looking boiled chicken, we politely declined and, to everyone's amusement, kept stuffing our faces with seafood. After days of plain village food, it was a feast to remember.

Fast forward around a decade. I had learned Chinese and lived in the country for several years; I had also begun cooking Chinese food with a passion and discovered the beauty of the late Anthony Bourdain's food and travel documentaries (which laid the groundwork for what I am trying to achieve with my channel, this book, and everything else I do). In those, he frequently brings up Hainanese chicken rice, a classic from Singapore with roots in the Hainanese city of Wenchang. Wait, did he say Wenchang? I've been there, around 10 years ago! And this is when it hit me.

That one night Mr. Sanchez took me and my friend to a Hainanese wedding, the night I remembered for the epic seafood feast, I completely missed the actual highlight: a taste of the real-deal Wenchang chicken. That was the dish that the locals kept trying to get us to eat and that we had nonchalantly declined.

Granted, I am not sure if we would have liked it. Fresh shrimp, clams, squid, lobster, and ocean fish are rare finds in Germany, especially if you don't have the money to spend on them. In Hainan, seafood practically grows on trees. Chicken, on the other hand, is a prized delicacy—especially the corn-fed, free-range chickens roaming freely around villages much like the one we had been staying in. For people from Hainan, the experience could have happened exactly like this, but in reverse.

Either way, I loved the irony in this benign but telling misunderstanding. In that moment, I not only made it a life goal to learn to appreciate Hainanese chicken rice—I vowed to perfect my home-cooked version of the dish. I now see it as the absolute best way to use a quality chicken and have traveled not just to Singapore but also back to Wenchang, Hainan for the sole purpose of fully appreciating this dish I had almost missed out on.

I know some people will never see Hainanese chicken rice as more than a boiled chicken on rice, but I will forever consider it a delicious reminder to see and learn about the world and its food through the eyes of locals.

EASY PLOV
(UZBEK RICE PILAF)

SERVES
1-2

PREP TIME
10 minutes

COOK TIME
30 minutes

Tired of fried rice? Try making a real-deal Uzbek plov. The issue: making it at home is not as simple as it sounds. Although the dish has only four essential ingredients, Uzbeks have made a whole science out of it. And while the results speak for themselves, I believe this method gets you unexpectedly close to the original flavor while massively cutting back on complexity.

DIRECTIONS

1. In a 10-inch (25cm) nonstick skillet, heat the oil over high heat. When shimmering, add the beef. Sauté for 2 to 3 minutes until browned. Add the onion and stir-fry for 1 minute. Add the rice and stir-fry for 2 minutes. Add the carrot and stir-fry for 2 minutes more.

2. Reduce the heat to low, and add the garlic, pepper, cumin, paprika, salt, and MSG. Cook for 1 minute.

3. Add the water, cover tightly with a lid, and cook for 10 minutes over low heat. Stir well, cover again, and cook for 10 minutes more. Stir well again and taste the rice. If it's undercooked, stir in another ¼ cup water, cover, and cook for 2 minutes more. Serve topped with chopped parsley, if desired.

NOTE: For a more striking visual presentation and a nod to the traditional Uzbek preparation method, place a whole head of garlic in the middle of the pan before moving to step 3.

2 tbsp **neutral cooking oil**

7oz (200g) **thin-cut beef** (such as skirt steak), finely chopped

½ large **white onion,** diced

½ cup **short-grain white rice** (3.5oz / 100g), well rinsed

1 small **carrot,** peeled and diced

3 cloves **garlic,** minced (see note)

1 tsp freshly cracked **black pepper** (20 cracks)

1 tsp **ground cumin**

1 tsp **paprika**

½ tsp **salt**

¼ tsp **MSG**

¾ cup **water** (4.6oz / 130g)

¼ cup finely chopped **fresh parsley** (optional), to serve

GU LOU YUK
(HONG KONG-STYLE SWEET & SOUR CHICKEN)

SERVES
2

PREP TIME
15 minutes

COOK TIME
10 minutes

Sweet and sour pork is a beloved Chinese food classic around the world. Its origins can be traced to Cantonese cuisine, and countless eateries in Hong Kong offer their versions. This simplified recipe relies on store-bought chicken nuggets, eliminating the need for deep-frying at home and turning this dish from a messy affair into a 10-minute stir-fry. It's great on its own or as part of a larger Chinese dinner and can easily be scaled up to serve more people.

DIRECTIONS

1. If using frozen nuggets, prepare according to package instructions. Cut the nuggets in half and set aside. If using leftover nuggets, arrange on a parchment paper–lined baking sheet and reheat in a 400°F (200°C) oven for 10 to 15 minutes or until crispy. Cut the nuggets in half and set aside.

2. To make the sauce, in a small bowl, combine all ingredients. Stir until the sugar has mostly dissolved.

3. In a wok or large nonstick skillet, heat the oil over medium-high heat until shimmering. Add the onion and stir-fry for 20 seconds. Add the peppers and stir-fry for 1 minute. Add the chicken nuggets and pineapple and stir-fry for 30 seconds.

4. Give the sauce a quick stir and add to the wok. Stir-fry for 1 minute or until the sauce has fully thickened before transferring to a serving plate. Serve over steamed white rice, if desired.

NOTE: The red wine vinegar can be replaced with white rice vinegar or any other plain white vinegar.

6 oz (180g) **chicken nuggets** (frozen or leftover)

2 tbsp **neutral cooking oil**

1 medium **red onion,** cut into 1-inch (2.5cm) pieces

⅓ **red bell pepper** (1.8oz / 50g), cut into 1-inch (2.5cm) pieces

⅓ **yellow bell pepper** (1.8oz / 50g), cut into 1-inch (2.5cm) pieces

⅓ **green bell pepper** (1.8oz / 50g), cut into 1-inch (2.5cm) pieces

½ cup **canned pineapple chunks** (3.5oz / 100g), drained (reserve the juice)

Steamed **white rice** (optional), to serve

FOR THE SAUCE

¼ cup **ketchup** (2.1oz / 60g)

¼ cup **granulated sugar** (2.1oz / 60g)

3 tbsp **red wine vinegar** (1.2oz / 35g) (see note)

2 tsp **soy sauce**

2 tbsp reserved **pineapple juice** (1.1oz / 30g)

1 tsp **cornstarch**

¼ tsp **salt**

LOMO SALTADO
(PERUVIAN STIR-FRY)

SERVES

2

PREP TIME

30 minutes

COOK TIME

15 minutes

This Peruvian dish, one of the most popular ones in the entire country, perfectly showcases how deeply Chinese cooking has influenced a nation on the other side of the globe. Not only is this basically a wok-style beef, onion, and tomato stir-fry, it also features soy sauce. The fun part is that it is served not just with rice but also with fries. Does it get any better?

DIRECTIONS

1. Heat a wok over high heat. Add 2 tablespoons oil. When shimmering, incrementally add in the onion, scallion, and aji amarillo (or bell pepper). Stir-fry for 2 to 3 minutes until the vegetables are lightly charred. Transfer the vegetables to a plate and set aside.

2. Return the wok to the burner and add the remaining 2 tablespoons oil. When shimmering, add half of the steak and stir-fry for about 2 minutes until the meat is cooked on the outside and caramelized. Repeat for the remaining steak slices.

3. Return the vegetables to the wok and add the tomato wedges and ginger. Stir-fry for 1 minute. Add the pisco, soy sauce, and vinegar. Stir-fry for 2 minutes. Add the garlic and cilantro and stir-fry for 15 seconds.

4. Serve hot with rice and french fries on the side, if desired.

4 tbsp **neutral cooking oil,** divided

1 large **red onion,** cut into petals

1 **scallion,** cut into 1-inch (2.5cm) pieces

1 **aji amarillo** (Peruvian yellow chili pepper) or **orange bell pepper,** diced

10 oz (300g) **beef steak,** thinly sliced

1 large **plum tomato,** cut into 8 wedges

½ tbsp minced **fresh ginger**

2 tbsp **pisco** or **Chinese cooking wine**

2 tbsp **soy sauce**

1 tbsp **white vinegar** or **lime juice**

1 clove **garlic,** minced

3 tbsp chopped **fresh cilantro**

TO SERVE (OPTIONAL)

French fries (frozen fries are fine!)

Steamed **white rice**

PEKING DUCK CHICKEN WRAPS

SERVES
2

PREP TIME
20 minutes

COOK TIME
35 minutes

I've tried to make Peking duck at home so many times that it's not even funny. And I can confidently say, it's not worth it. But that doesn't mean you can't scratch that Peking duck itch in your home kitchen. And guess what? You don't need any fancy equipment—or even a duck, for that matter. Say hello to your new favorite wrap!

DIRECTIONS

1. Preheat the oven to 425°F (220°C). Line a baking sheet with foil.

2. In a large bowl, toss the drumsticks with the oil, five spice powder, salt, cornstarch, and baking powder until evenly seasoned.

3. Arrange the drumsticks on the prepared baking sheet, leaving space between them to cook evenly. Bake for 30 minutes or until golden brown. Flip halfway through cooking.

4. To make the sauce, in a small bowl, combine all ingredients.

5. Remove the drumsticks from the oven. When cool enough to handle, remove the meat from the bones and roughly chop into bite-sized pieces.

6. To assemble the wraps, apply a layer of sauce to each tortilla followed by half of the lettuce, leek, cucumber, cilantro, chicken, and lime juice. Roll tightly before serving.

NOTE: Save the unused leek greens for stock and leek whites for dumpling fillings—it's an underrated allium with a great flavor profile.

4 large **chicken drumsticks**

1 tbsp **neutral cooking oil**

1 tsp **five spice powder**

½ tsp **salt**

2 tsp **cornstarch**

½ tsp **baking powder**

2 large **whole wheat tortillas**

¼ medium head of **iceberg lettuce**, shredded

⅓ **leek**, light green part only, finely sliced lengthwise (see note)

½ **English cucumber**, julienned

2 sprigs **fresh cilantro**, leaves only

Juice of ½ **lime**

FOR THE SAUCE

¼ cup **hoisin sauce**

1½ tbsp **honey**

½ tbsp **soy sauce**

½ tsp **white pepper**

½ tsp **sesame oil**

Sauces & Condiments

Almost every dish can be made a bit more exciting with a little drizzle of the right sauce. This is hardly a secret, and clearly every single culture in the world has uncovered the magic powers of the sauce. Many will even have that one sauce or condiment they eat with absolutely everything. This chapter is all about these little dabs of joy!

Chili Crisp **204**

Chiu Chow Chili Oil **205**

Sweet Chili Sauce **207**

Green Chutney **210**

Red Chutney **211**

Obazda **213**

Kuya Rafa's Sawsawan Dip **215**

Svanetian Salt **218**

Chimichurri **221**

Ginger Scallion Crisp **223**

Semi-Salted Dill Pickles **226**

Russian Sauerkraut **227**

Condiments: the Secret Sauce

Never underestimate the power of condiments. If you want to add extra heat, extra tang, or extra richness, a little sauce on the side never hurts. In fact, more often than I'd like to admit, a well-paired sauce might overshadow the main meal itself.

SPICING IT UP

In recent years, Chinese-style **chili crisp** has taken the internet and foodie culture by storm. Not only is it easy to make in large batches (a perfect present for like-minded foodie friends, by the way!), it also is extremely satisfying to do so and will go with pretty much everything. Yes, that even goes for dessert. In its home country of China, chili crisp is the first (and sometimes only) thing any student would need to slap on some rice or instant noodles during long nights of cramming.

There is, however, an underdog competitor to the more popular Sichuan-style chili crisp, which is **Chiu Chow chili oil.** Named after a Chinese city with very distinct traditions both culturally as well as culinarily, its origins couldn't be further from its Sichuanese cousin. This condiment focuses more on savory, almost sweet notes from roasted garlic and ginger as well as a fruity note from the addition of not just dried but also fresh chilies.

Speaking of sweetness—I always loved how spiciness paired with it. Which is probably why I loved **sweet chili sauce** before I knew what chilies even were. The recipe in this chapter offers a homemade alternative to the store-bought stuff, and you'd be surprised how easy it is to work with!

If you jealously look on as your friends enjoy chili crisp but just don't have the tolerance for spiciness, I might have just the solution for you: **ginger scallion crisp.** It utilizes the same techniques as some of its chili-packed relatives but yields a fragrant, addictive condiment that hits a proud zero on the Scoville scale.

TRAVEL DIPS

Of course, condiments do not stop at chili sauce; in fact, we have barely scratched the surface. Let's face it, when it comes to sauces, we can simply not leave Indian cuisine unmentioned. Many of the curries and gravies that have started to grow in popularity across the world are essentially one big sauce with things in it—just choose your vehicle of choice to mop them up and enjoy. Indian chefs are true masters of sauce. But even in a sauce-based cuisine, there are more sauces: I am talking about **chutneys.** That subcategory alone is a rabbit hole you can go down, but you can get started with the two basic recipes in this chapter.

I would also like to bring your attention to **chimichurri,** one of the simplest but also most rewarding sauces I have ever had. Born as a simple Argentinian cattle ranchers' recipe, it convinced me the first time I added a drop of it on some freshly grilled beef. While, like many sauces, it goes incredibly well with more things than I could ever list here, it particularly shines as a companion to steak or other barbecued meat. But if I may suggest one more use for it: brush it on slices of bread and briefly toast them in the oven—it's going to give garlic bread a run for its money.

If you are looking for an even simpler way to add some pizzazz to your dishes, let's take a quick detour to the Caucasus, namely the country of Georgia. The nation boasts a unique cuisine that combines Persian, Russian, and Middle Eastern influences. Among the many eye-opening techniques and ingredients you can discover is **Svanetian salt.** A jar of this spiced salt could last for years—but I promise it won't.

THE CREAMY AND THE CRUNCHY

I also want to leave you with two condiments from my home countries of Germany and Russia that slightly break the mold. The first one is a funky, rich, and creamy Bavarian spread called **obazda.** It is a bit funny to me (and most other Germans for that matter) that when people speak of German food, they are usually talking about Bavarian food, but not even in a way that would represent it well. I suggest we start working on this right now, so how about you try my obazda recipe the next time you are looking for something to go with a warm pretzel or a fresh loaf of sourdough? It's what beer cheese dreams of being.

Last but not least, may I offer you a pickle? I know, I know—this is not a sauce, but I think it passes as a condiment. Also I am not simply giving you a recipe for a dill pickle. Instead, this recipe is for **Russian semi-salted pickles,** which sit right between a pickle and a fresh cucumber. Sounds strange? Try them and you will understand why Russians go absolutely crazy over them.

CHILI CRISP

MAKES
2½ cups

PREP TIME
10 minutes

COOK TIME
30 minutes

There aren't many foods that aren't improved by a generous drizzle of chili crisp. The flavor is deeply complex, with the different aromas coming through as you eat. But it doesn't end at flavor: the slightly crunchy texture of the toasted chili flakes is complemented perfectly by the smoothness of the oil.

DIRECTIONS

1. In a large wok over medium heat, toast the bay leaves, star anise, cinnamon, cardamom, fennel seeds, Sichuan peppercorns, ginger, and garlic until fragrant.

2. Add the oil to the wok and continue to cook for about 15 minutes until the oil is infused and the garlic is golden. Remove and discard the aromatics.

3. Add the shallots, peanuts, preserved mustard greens, and fermented black bean paste to the wok. Reduce the heat to medium-low and cook for 3 to 5 minutes or until the shallot begins to turn golden brown.

4. In a heat safe medium bowl, combine the chili flakes, salt, sugar, and MSG.

5. Pour the infused hot oil through a strainer and into the bowl in three additions, stirring to coat the chili flakes in between pours. Right before the last pour, add the sesame seeds and vinegar. Place in the refrigerator to cool for 15 minutes.

6. When cool, transfer to a resealable jar and let sit on the counter overnight. Store in the refrigerator and consume within 2 weeks. Stir well and apply liberally to just about anything—including vanilla ice cream!

2 **bay leaves**

3 **star anise pods**

2 small **cinnamon sticks**

3 **black cardamom pods**

½ tbsp **fennel seeds**

1 tbsp whole **Sichuan peppercorns**

5 slices **fresh ginger**

5 cloves **garlic**, smashed

2 cups **neutral cooking oil** (16oz / 500g)

2 **shallots**, finely minced

½ cup **roasted and salted peanuts**, finely chopped or crushed

¼ cup minced **Sichuanese preserved mustard greens** (optional)

2 tbsp **fermented black bean paste**

1½ cups **red chili flakes** (7.1oz / 200g)

2 tsp **salt**

1 tbsp **granulated sugar**

1 tsp **MSG**

¼ cup **sesame seeds**

2 tbsp **dark Chinese vinegar**

CHIU CHOW CHILI OIL

MAKES
1⅓ cups

PREP TIME
10 minutes

COOK TIME
15–30 minutes

While chili crisp stands out due to its complexity and depth of flavor, Chiu Chow chili oil is an entirely different beast. Rich in lightly toasted garlic, it provides much more umami and sweetness, paired with a fruity note from the addition of fresh chilies. If you thought chili crisp was addictive, try this.

DIRECTIONS

1. To a small nonstick skillet, add the peanut oil, fresh red chilies, ginger, and garlic. Bring to a gentle simmer over medium-low heat.

2. Simmer for 15 to 20 minutes or until the garlic begins to turn golden brown and the oil has almost stopped bubbling. Stir occasionally to prevent sticking.

3. Stir in the chili flakes, sugar, salt, and MSG. Bring to a gentle simmer for 7 minutes.

4. Stir in the soy sauce, vinegar, and sesame oil. Simmer for 1 minute more.

5. Remove from the heat and cool completely before transferring to a sterilized, sealable container for storage. The chili oil can be refrigerated for up to 1 week. Enjoy on everything.

NOTES: The availability of chili peppers varies widely across the world. For the fresh chilies, use whatever you like, as long as it's red and a pepper. Anything from habanero for spicy to bell pepper for mild. Try to find seedless chili flakes. I like using the Korean kind (*gochugaru*).

You may want to adjust the amount of oil, depending on what ratio of oil to solids you prefer. The oil is smoother and milder. The solids are concentrated in flavor and textured.

If you can't grate the ginger and garlic, pulse in a food processor until finely chopped.

¾ cup **peanut oil** or **neutral cooking oil** (7.1oz / 200g)

4 medium **fresh red chilies** (1.8oz / 50g), finely minced (see note)

1-inch (2.5cm) piece **fresh ginger,** grated

20–24 cloves **garlic,** finely minced or grated

¼ cup **red chili flakes** (1.1oz / 30g) (see note)

1 tbsp **sugar** (brown or granulated)

1 tsp **salt**

½ tsp **MSG**

1 tbsp **light soy sauce**

½ tbsp **apple cider vinegar** or **rice vinegar**

½ tbsp **toasted sesame oil**

SWEET CHILI SAUCE

MAKES
2 cups

PREP TIME
5 minutes

COOK TIME
10 minutes + 2 hours to chill

Name one deep-fried food that doesn't taste better dipped in sweet chili sauce. Tangy, sweet, and spicy with a generous note of garlic, it simply never disappoints.

DIRECTIONS

1. In a small food processor, combine the lime juice, fresh red chilies, chili flakes, shallot, garlic, ginger, and salt. Blend for about 1 minute until you get fine chunks but before everything becomes a paste. (This can also be done using an immersion blender.)

2. Transfer the mixture to a medium saucepan. Place over medium-high heat, add the vinegar and sugar, and bring to a boil. When boiling, reduce the heat to low and simmer for 5 minutes.

3. In a small bowl, combine the starch and water to make a slurry. Immediately add to the saucepan and stir in. Bring the mixture to a simmer and cook for 1 minute.

4. Transfer the sauce to a resealable jar, and refrigerate for 2 hours before using. The sauce can be stored in the refrigerator for at least 2 weeks.

NOTE: You can use whatever chilies you prefer—anything from a bell pepper to the hottest chili you can find will work. It's mostly about your own preference and local availability. Deseeding the chilies is highly recommended.

½ cup **lime juice**

14 oz (400g) mixed **fresh red chilies** (see note)

1 tbsp **red chili flakes**

1 **shallot**

3 cloves **garlic**

1-inch (2.5cm) piece **fresh ginger**

1½ tsp **salt**

1 cup **white vinegar**

1½ cups **granulated sugar**

2 tbsp **tapioca starch** or **cornstarch**

¼ cup **water**

GREEN CHUTNEY

MAKES
1¼ cups

PREP TIME
5 minutes

COOK TIME
10 minutes + 1 hour to cool

One of the most irresistible parts of Indian cuisine is the richness of the many layers of flavor. A chutney is a great way to bring some of this aromatic depth to any meal you like in the form of an easy-to-use condiment. This green chutney adds a refreshing herbal note to any dish and is a perfect balance for any fried food among other things!

DIRECTIONS

1. To a 5-inch saucepan, add the butter, mustard seeds, curry leaves, garam masala, curry powder, and mung dal. Heat over medium heat for 3 minutes or until butter has fully melted and the spices begin to sizzle and smell fragrant.

2. Stir in the ginger, onion, garlic, and green chili. Sauté for 2 more minutes. Add the water, bring to a simmer, and cook for 1 minute. Allow the mixture to cool for 5 to 10 minutes.

3. Transfer the cooled mixture to a small food processor. Add the cilantro, mint, peanuts, sugar, salt, MSG, and lime juice. Blend for 2 minutes or until smooth.

4. Transfer to an airtight container and refrigerate for at least 1 hour before use. Chutney can be refrigerated for up to 5 days.

4 tbsp clarified **butter** (1.8oz / 50g)

1 tsp **brown mustard seeds**

5 **curry leaves**

½ tsp **garam masala**

1 tsp **curry powder**

1 tbsp **mung dal**

1-inch (2.5cm) piece **fresh ginger**, chopped

½ large **onion**, chopped

2 cloves **garlic**, roughly chopped

1 **fresh green chili**, chopped

1 cup **water**

1 cup chopped **fresh cilantro** (2.5oz / 70g), packed

¼ cup chopped **fresh mint** (0.7oz / 20g), packed

3 tbsp **roasted and salted peanuts** (1oz / 30g)

2 tbsp **granulated sugar**

1 tsp **salt**

¼ tsp **MSG**

1½ tbsp **lime juice**

RED CHUTNEY

MAKES
2 cups

PREP TIME
5 minutes

COOK TIME
7 minutes + 1 hour to cool

If green chutney is the yin, this red chutney is the yang. It adds warmth and intensity to more mellow dishes. You can even top a simple bowl of rice or mashed potatoes with it, and I promise you won't be disappointed.

DIRECTIONS

1. To a small saucepan, add the butter, mustard seeds, curry leaves, garam masala, cumin, chili flakes, tomato paste, and mung dal. Place over medium heat for 4 minutes or until the butter has fully melted and the spice mix begins to sizzle and smells fragrant.

2. Stir in the ginger, onion, and garlic. Sauté for 2 minutes. Add the water, bring to a simmer, and cook for 1 minute.

3. Remove from the heat and let the mixture cool for 5 to 10 minutes. Transfer to a small food processor. Add the sugar, salt, MSG, and lime juice. Blend for 2 minutes or until smooth.

4. Transfer to an airtight container and refrigerate for at least 1 hour before use. Chutney can be refrigerated for up to 5 days.

4 tbsp clarified **butter** (1.8oz / 50g)

1 tsp **brown mustard seeds**

5 **curry leaves**

1 tsp **garam masala**

1 tsp **ground cumin**

1 tbsp **red chili flakes**

2 tbsp **tomato paste**

2 tbsp **mung dal**

½-inch (1.25cm) piece **fresh ginger**, chopped

½ large **onion**, chopped

2 cloves **garlic,** roughly chopped

½ cup **water**

1 tsp **granulated sugar**

1 tsp **salt**

¼ tsp **MSG**

½ tbsp **lime juice**

OBAZDA
(BAVARIAN CHEESE SPREAD)

MAKES
¾ cup

PREP TIME
5 minutes

COOK TIME
None

Online, I frequently stumble upon people dipping pretzels in mustard. It's not wrong per se, but it is my opinion that mustard is for sausages, while pretzels are dipped in something much better: obazda. This spread, traditionally made from mature cheese, goes exceptionally well with them. Just make sure to get all ingredients out of the fridge an hour before you start cooking. Thank me later!

DIRECTIONS

1. In a medium bowl, use a fork to mash together all ingredients until well combined.

2. Transfer the mixture to a serving bowl and garnish with a pinch of smoked paprika and chives. Enjoy as part of a traditional Bavarian appetizer spread with soft pretzels, sliced meats, and pickles, and wash it down with a beer.

NOTE: If the rind of the Camembert is not soft enough to be mashed with a fork, use your hand.

4 oz (125g) mature **Camembert** or **Brie,** at room temperature (see note)

1 oz (30g) softened **butter**

3 oz (85g) **cream cheese,** at room temperature

1 small **shallot,** minced

1 tbsp finely chopped **fresh chives**

1 tsp **ground caraway**

1 tsp **smoked paprika,** plus more to garnish

Salt and freshly cracked **black pepper,** to taste

1 tbsp **beer**

2 tsp **apple cider vinegar**

Pinch of **sugar**

Choped **fresh chives,** to garnish

KUYA RAFA'S
SAWSAWAN DIP

MAKES
1 cup

PREP TIME
5 minutes + 1 hour to chill

COOK TIME
None

My friend Rafa whipped up this dip as I was testing my lumpia recipe (page 64). What took him mere minutes to make turned out so well that we decided it simply had to be included in this book. Like most of the condiments here, it will go well with many dishes, especially when you want to brighten up fatty and savory dishes.

DIRECTIONS

1. In a small bowl, combine the onion, cilantro, and chilies. Add the soy sauce, vinegar, and Sprite. Mix well.

2. Transfer to an airtight container and refrigerate for at least 1 hour before consuming. Can be stored in the refrigerator for up to 5 days.

1 **white onion,** finely diced

¼ cup finely chopped **fresh cilantro**

2 **fresh Thai red chilies** or other small chilies, thinly sliced

¼ cup **soy sauce**

¼ cup **white vinegar**

¼ cup **Sprite** or other lemon-lime soda

One Dip to Rule Them All

Starting a food channel on YouTube is not a joke. The first time I set up a camera and filmed a recipe, it took me days to shoot and put together. I knew the result wasn't a masterpiece, but you gotta start somewhere, right? After all this work, I uploaded the video to YouTube to see it receive a whopping 50 views, mostly from the friends I shared it with. *Great,* I thought, *now I have to do this every week until the end of time, waiting for my channel to magically explode. Isn't this how YouTube works?*

Jokes aside, the first months, maybe years of running a YouTube channel are a special time. You upload videos to a tiny but dedicated base of followers who share your passion. You memorize the names of your commenters, your conversations span across video comment sections, and you may even meet some in the flesh. Although you know the numbers don't even remotely add up to call it anything but a labor of love, this is where you have the chance to understand how an audience member sees your videos on an individual level. I tried to keep track of everyone's success who publicly shared making one of my recipes. Those anecdotes of people's dinner parties, weeknight meals, and special gatherings involving recipes I developed in my own dimly lit kitchen late at night were what kept me going before I ever imagined calling my channel my job.

This is one of these stories, and it comes from one of my longtime best friends, who was also one of the first supporters of the channel. He and his wife were once invited to an unconventional wedding held in a remote, rustic outdoor setting. With little time to prepare a wedding gift, in a last-minute effort, they whipped up an enormous batch of my Chiu Chow Chili Oil (page 205) for the bride and groom.

The wedding itself, set in a beautiful location, was as unusual and beautiful as expected. At the center of the feast that followed was a spectacular spit roast, with dozens of salivating party guests gathered around it as it slowly cooked over a crackling bonfire. The hosts had thought of everything—or should I say, nearly everything. With plates full of smoky and succulent meat, the wedding guests were missing one thing: just a little sauce. But alas, there was none to be found.

But then it hit them: there was a huge tub of chili oil. Minutes later, the jar was getting passed around and big dollops of the fragrant, bright red paste started appearing on every single plate.

I was not there, but according to eye witness accounts, the chili oil became the star of the show. Not only was it fantastic with the food (although admittedly, it's fantastic with almost anything), it was also the missing piece that added a little story to an already unforgettable night.

For those who ask what kept me going when it felt like no one was watching my videos, it was moments like this that did it. There could be a story like this behind every single view.

SVANETIAN SALT

MAKES
1 cup

PREP TIME
5 minutes + 1 hour to cool

COOK TIME
90 minutes

In Georgia (the country!), you will find some form of this seasoned salt in every household. It's a fantastically simple way to sprinkle extra flavor over almost any dish. Normally made from a range of local ingredients, I realized you can get a very similar flavor and easily cut your ingredient list in half by going for that jar of unused curry powder in your cupboard.

6 large cloves **garlic**, smashed

⅓ cup **sea salt**

2 tbsp **curry powder**

3 tbsp **sweet paprika**

⅓ cup roughly chopped **fresh dill** (about 3 large stalks)

DIRECTIONS

1. Preheat the oven to 170°F (75°C). Line a baking sheet with parchment paper.

2. In a food processor, combine all the ingredients and process until the mixture is well combined and similar to wet sand in texture.

3. Spread the salt mixture evenly on the prepared baking sheet. Place in the oven to dry for about 90 minutes or until most of the moisture has evaporated.

4. Remove from the oven and allow to cool and continue drying for at least 1 hour. Return the salt mixture to the food processor and process for about 2 minutes or until very fine.

CHIMICHURRI

MAKES
¾ cup

PREP TIME
5 minutes + 3 hours to rest

COOK TIME
None

If you are looking for a bright, tangy, and herbal sauce that's easy to make—look no further. Chimichurri is here to save the day. Traditionally a condiment for Argentinian beef steaks, it is also a fantastic focaccia topping or dip!

DIRECTIONS

1. To a food processor, add all ingredients. Pulse for 20 seconds or until fully combined.

2. Transfer to an airtight container and let sit for at least 3 hours before using to give the flavor time to develop. Refrigerate for up to 10 days.

NOTE: Olive oil will solidify in the fridge. Let the chimichurri rest at room temperature for 30 to 60 minutes (or heat in the microwave for 15 seconds) before use.

½ cup **extra virgin olive oil** (3.9oz / 110g)

2 tbsp **red wine vinegar** (1.1oz / 30g)

1 **shallot,** roughly chopped

½ cup roughly chopped **fresh parsley** (1.2oz / 35g), packed

1 clove **garlic,** crushed

1 **red jalapeño,** deseeded and roughly chopped

1 tsp **dried oregano**

½ tsp **salt,** or to taste

¼ tsp **granulated sugar**

½ tsp freshly cracked **black pepper** (20 cracks), or to taste

GINGER SCALLION CRISP

MAKES
1½ cups

PREP TIME
10 minutes + 20 minutes to cool

COOK TIME
20-25 minutes

One time I wanted to make chili crisp but, embarrassingly, forgot to buy chili flakes. I did, however, have enormous amounts of everything else, so naturally I wondered: what if I skipped chili crisp's titular ingredient? Out came this recipe for ginger scallion crisp. The blondie to the chili crisp brownie, so to speak. And believe me, this is every bit as good as its cousin!

DIRECTIONS

1. To a food processor, add the scallions, ginger, garlic, cooking oil, salt, MSG, sugar, and soy sauce. Pulse for 20 to 30 seconds until finely chopped.

2. Transfer the mixture to a cold 8-inch (20cm) nonstick skillet. Place over medium heat and simmer for 20 to 25 minutes, stirring frequently, until the solids go from a paste to individual pieces and just begin to turn golden brown. Remove from the heat and cool in the skillet for 20 minutes. (The solids should turn golden brown as they cool.)

3. Stir in the sesame oil before transferring to a lidded glass jar. Refrigerate for up to 10 days.

5 **scallions**, roughly chopped

2-inch (5cm) piece **fresh ginger,** roughly chopped

2 cloves **garlic,** peeled

1¼ cup **neutral cooking oil** (9.7oz / 275g)

1 tsp **salt**

1 tsp **MSG**

2 tsp **brown sugar**

1 tbsp **soy sauce**

½ tbsp **sesame oil**

SEMI-SALTED DILL PICKLES

MAKES
Two 1-quart jars

PREP TIME
20 minutes

COOK TIME
5 minutes + 48 hours to rest

There are many different types of pickles out there, but I really feel like the world is missing out on one type in particular: the semi-salted pickle of Eastern Europe. Born out of laziness (probably), this variety is only fermented briefly, resulting in a dill pickle–like exterior layer with the "heart" of a fresh cucumber. The best of both worlds, so to speak!

2 lb (900g) small **pickling cucumbers**

6 cups **water** (1.5L)

¼ cup **salt** (2.6oz / 75g)

1 cup **fresh dill** (0.9oz / 25g), divided

4 cloves **garlic**, crushed

6 **radishes**, halved

1 **jalapeño**, sliced

1 tbsp **mustard seeds**

DIRECTIONS

1. Trim about ½ inch (1.25cm) off both ends of the cucumbers.

2. In a saucepan, combine the water and salt and bring to a boil over high heat. Cook for 1 to 2 minutes or until the salt has fully dissolved. Set aside.

3. Wash and sterilize two 1-quart canning jars. Into each jar, pack ¼ cup dill, 1 garlic clove, 6 radish halves, half of the jalapeño slices, and ½ tablespoon mustard seeds.

4. Into each jar, tightly pack as many cucumbers as possible. To the top of each jar, add ¼ cup dill and 1 garlic clove.

5. Stir the pickling liquid to make sure the salt is completely dissolved. Carefully pour the liquid over the contents of each jar, filling it all the way. Be sure the cucumbers are packed tightly enough to stay submerged. (Discard excess salted water if needed.)

6. Seal and let sit on the counter for 24 hours. After that, transfer the jars to the refrigerator for 24 to 48 hours before consuming. Refrigerate for up to 10 days.

RUSSIAN SAUERKRAUT

MAKES
4 cups

PREP TIME
20 minutes

COOK TIME
3 days to ferment

Every Russian family will have a tub of this simple fermented cabbage somewhere in the back of the fridge. What really makes a difference is adding some extra sugar after the first round of fermentation. It not only improves the flavor but also adds a mild effervescence over time.

1⅓ lb (600g) shredded **green cabbage** (about ½ small head)

7 oz (200g) thinly julienned **carrot** (2-3 carrots)

1 tbsp **salt**

1 tbsp **granulated sugar**

DIRECTIONS

1. Sterilize a 1-quart (1 liter) glass pickling jar and lid.

2. In a large bowl, toss the cabbage and carrots with the salt. Use your hands to mix and massage thoroughly.

3. Pack the mixture into the prepared jar. Add room temperature water to fill the jar, leaving about 1½ to 2 inches (3–4cm) of headspace.

4. Seal the jar and let sit for 3 to 5 days at room temperature, out of direct sunlight. Make sure the veggies remain fully submerged in the liquid. "Burp" the sauerkraut every day by briefly opening and resealing the jar to release pressure.

5. When small bubbles appear in the jar and the cabbage begins to smell tangy, mix in the sugar, add more water if needed to keep the vegetables submerged, and refrigerate overnight. Sauerkraut is now ready to eat and can be kept refrigerated for at least 2 weeks.

Drinks & Desserts

It's always fun to sweeten up your meal. We all know sugar should be consumed in moderation, but when we indulge, it better be worth it! No matter if you want something to go with an otherwise savory meal or just a little treat for yourself, I hope this chapter provides some inspiration.

Russian Syrniki Muffins **233**

Churros **235**

Better Than Fanta **237**

Dulce de Leche, Easy Mode **240**

Salted Caramel Sauce **241**

Suan Mei Tang **245**

Banana Bread **247**

Chocolate "Potatoes" **249**

Drinks & Desserts: the Cherry on Top

"Dessert is like a feel-good song and the best ones make you dance." I wish I could remember where I heard this quote, but I couldn't agree more.

BOTTOMS UP

I have a confession to make: I have an addiction to sparkling water. I'm not even joking. Germany has by far the highest sparkling water per capita consumption in the world, and it has definitely shaped my drinking habits. I consume it daily (no exceptions), and whenever I arrive in a new country, one of the first things I do is find a place that sells sparkling water. I will purchase it at any cost.

Fortunately, it's one of the least damaging habits you could possibly have, at least as long as I stick to water. In the summer months though, my habit will admittedly extend to drinking soda, one of my guilty pleasures. It does, however, feel a little better when that soda is homemade. As long as you have some sparkling water to work with, all you gotta do is make a syrup and mix the two to your liking. I am sharing my recipe for homemade **Fanta** in this chapter, but this should really just be a starting point for you. The world of DIY soda knows absolutely no bounds!

Another drink recipe I'm sharing is for a Chinese drink you have probably never heard of: **suan mei tang,** or sour plum juice. I first tried this drink on a blistering-hot summer day in China. I was sweating profusely, and my local friends convinced me it was exactly what I needed. The reason? Suan mei tang is not just a drink; it's traditional Chinese medicine. Its properties are said to cool you down internally—and even if it might be thanks to the placebo effect, I feel like it really works! A little caveat: the ingredients could be hard to source. But if you have a Chinatown nearby (or are a savvy online shopper) and struggle with summer heat, it may very well be worth a try.

SWEET DREAMS ARE MADE OF THIS

I am generally a person who eats nearly everything. Very few foods in the world make me say "no." One of those, however, is the banana. I simply don't understand what makes people like this chalky, overly sweet stick of goop. Which is why one day I challenged myself: can I find one, just one, way of eating bananas I enjoy? The answer is yes: **banana bread.** I scoured the internet and collected and tried all the tips I could find. Some didn't do much; some made a huge difference. In the end, out came my recipe, and I can now proudly say I conquered the banana.

The banana bread tastes great by itself, but it only gets better when you drizzle it with some **salted caramel sauce.** That recipe in itself is not exactly something I discovered traveling but is rather something I think should be in every home cook's repertoire. If you happen to be intimidated by cooking caramel at home, don't fret. There is actually an old-school technique where you magically turn a can of sweetened condensed milk into the simplest possible **dulce de leche,** a thick and creamy sauce tasting of dairy and caramel.

Both of these are incredible with **churros,** by the way. While they're traditionally dipped in chocolate sauce, I think milky caramel is the way to go—which I learned on the streets of Lima, Peru.

RUSSIAN DELIGHTS

I could never talk about dessert without mentioning Russian dessert culture. People really do have a sweet tooth in Russia, which is evident in their sugar-laden cups of tea. Something you'll often find served with tea are **syrniki,** sweet little pan-fried pancakes made from cottage cheese. My Grandma Tata makes (hands down) the best ones and was glad to share her recipe, but there was a

problem: two of the most important ingredients, Russian *tvorog* (cottage cheese) and *manka* (a special type of flour) are extremely hard to come by globally. It took me many attempts to find a workaround, but with the help of ricotta cheese and a muffin pan, you should be able to whip these up pretty much anywhere in the world.

And finally, my family favorite: the **chocolate potato.** Originally an ingenious method of using leftover cookies and cake trimmings in the tightly managed Soviet food production system, chocolate potatoes quickly became a widely known trick utilized by homekeepers to make use of their scraps as well. If you don't mind the copious amounts of butter and sugar in there, this is a bite of simple but decadent Soviet dessert culture you will be dreaming of for weeks.

RUSSIAN SYRNIKI MUFFINS

MAKES
6 syrniki

PREP TIME
10 minutes

COOK TIME
30 minutes

My grandma is famous for her mouthwatering *syrniki,* a very common Russian snack that can be best described as something between a cheesecake and a pancake. Adapting her recipe into a version that works with globally available ingredients was no easy task, but I think I did it. Enjoy these with a cup of tea any time of the day!

DIRECTIONS

1. Lightly grease the cups of a 6-cup muffin pan with butter. Preheat the oven to 350°F (180°C).

2. In a medium bowl, whisk together the ricotta, flour, sugar, lemon juice, apple cider vinegar, egg, vanilla, cinnamon, and salt until well combined.

3. Fill each cup of the muffin pan halfway with batter.

4. Bake on the middle rack for 25 to 30 minutes or until golden brown on top. Rest for 5 to 10 minutes before turning out of the pan. (You may need to run a knife or offset spatula around the edge to loosen.)

5. Serve each sirnik with a dollop of sour cream and jam.

NOTE: If you have trouble sourcing soft wheat flour, mix 3 parts semolina and 1 part cornstarch for a substitute flour.

2 tsp **butter,** to grease pan

9 oz (250g) **full-fat ricotta**

⅓ cup **farina soft wheat flour**

3 tbsp **granulated sugar**

¼ cup **lemon juice**

2 tbsp **apple cider vinegar**

1 **egg**

½ tsp **vanilla extract**

¼ tsp **ground cinnamon**

⅛ tsp **salt**

TO SERVE

6 tbsp **sour cream**

6 tsp **strawberry jam** or other jam

CHURROS

MAKES
15-25 churros

PREP TIME
20 minutes

COOK TIME
20 minutes

There aren't many desserts worth going through the hassle of deep frying at home, but churros are among the few. You can always have them with hot chocolate (and even dip them into it), as per tradition. But for a sweet treat truly out of this world, try them with my Salted Caramel Sauce (page 241)!

DIRECTIONS

1. Prepare the coating by combining the sugar and cinnamon in a tray.

2. In a medium bowl, combine the flour, brown sugar, and ½ cup milk. Whisk until it becomes a stiff dough. Add the remaining ½ cup milk, and whisk until completely combined.

3. In a small nonstick skillet over medium-low heat, melt the butter. When melted, add to the dough. Using a spatula, stir constantly for 2 minutes until fully incorporated. When done, place in the refrigerator for about 10 minutes to cool.

4. While the dough is cooling, preheat the oil to 360°F (180°C) in a deep fryer or large Dutch oven.

5. In a large bowl, combine the cooled dough, egg, and vanilla. Mix together until homogenous. Transfer to a piping bag fitted with a ½-inch (1.25cm) rounded star tip.

6. Carefully pipe 6-inch (15cm) segments of the mixture into the preheated oil. Cut the end with clean scissors. The process works best if you hold the bag in your nondominant hand over the oil, apply pressure with the same hand, and have the scissors ready in your dominant hand.

7. Deep-fry for 5 to 6 minutes on both sides or until deeply golden brown. Transfer to paper towels to drain excess oil for about 2 minutes. Once drained, immediately toss the fried dough in the coating, turning until completely coated. Serve warm.

1 cup **all-purpose flour** (4.9oz / 140g)

1 tbsp **brown sugar** (0.5oz / 15g)

1 cup **milk** (8.6oz / 245g), divided

½ stick **butter** (2.1oz / 60g), cut into small cubes

1 large **egg**

½ tsp **vanilla extract**

Vegetable oil, for frying (about 4 cups or 1 liter)

FOR COATING
5 tbsp **granulated sugar**
½ tsp **ground cinnamon**

BETTER THAN FANTA

MAKES
2 cups syrup

PREP TIME
10 minutes

COOK TIME
2 minutes + 1 hour to chill

Once you start making your own syrups for DIY soda, you might never go back. Start with this basic Fanta recipe (and trust me, the tangerine juice is a game changer), and experiment from there by adding your favorite spices, fruit juices, and whatever else your inner child desires!

DIRECTIONS

1. Add the orange juice and tangerine juice to a 2-cup liquid measuring cup. Add water to reach 1¼ cups (300ml) of liquid. (If you have more than 1¼ cups of juice to start, reduce as needed.)

2. In a small saucepan, combine the juice, sugar, orange zest, and lemon zest. Bring to a simmer over medium heat and cook for 2 minutes.

3. Turn off the heat. If desired, add a few drops of red food coloring to achieve a very deep orange color. Stir in the citric acid and salt. Let the mixture cool and infuse on the counter for at least 1 to 4 hours or refrigerate overnight.

4. Strain through a fine sieve into a resealable bottle. Squeeze out as much liquid as possible from the zest. The syrup can be stored in the refrigerator for 2 weeks.

5. To use, dissolve 1 tablespoon of the syrup in a little bit of sparkling water. Then slowly add more fresh sparkling water to taste. Add ice cubes, if desired.

3 **oranges** (zest and juice, zest finely minced)

Juice of 2 **tangerines**

2 cups **granulated sugar** (14oz / 400g)

Zest of 1 **lemon,** finely minced

Red food coloring (optional)

¼ oz (7.5g) **citric acid**

⅛ tsp **salt**

TO SERVE
Cold **sparkling water**
Ice cubes (optional)

DULCE DE LECHE, EASY MODE

MAKES
1 can

PREP TIME
1 minute

COOK TIME
3 hours + 1 hour to cool

This is guaranteed to be the easiest recipe for *dulce de leche*—a rich and creamy, caramel-like spread—you have ever seen. Don't believe me? Look at the ingredient list. As long as you follow a few basic safety precautions, this genius method will undoubtedly become part of your dessert repertoire!

1 can **sweetened condensed milk** (any size)

DIRECTIONS

1. Remove the wrapper from the can and place the unopened can on its side in a large pot or Dutch oven. Fill the pot with water, adding enough so that the can is completely submerged and the water level is at least 2 inches (5cm) above the can. (The can must remain completely submerged throughout the cooking process to prevent warping and splitting.)

2. Place over medium heat, cover with a lid, and simmer for 3 hours. Check the water level occasionally, making sure the can remains fully submerged. Add more water if needed to maintain a water level of 2 inches (5cm) above the can at all times.

3. Using tongs, carefully remove the can from the hot water and place it on a kitchen towel to cool for at least 1 hour. Do not attempt to open the can until it has cooled to room temperature. Attempting to open the can before it has completely cooled can result in the contents exploding.

4. Transfer to a resealable container for storage, and enjoy on anything as a sweet spread. Refrigerate for up to 5 days.

SALTED CARAMEL SAUCE

MAKES
1¼ cups

PREP TIME
3 minutes

COOK TIME
10 minutes

Sometimes all you need for a moment of happiness is a spoonful of salted caramel sauce—so here is my recipe. Drizzle it over desserts, dip fruit or cookies in it, stuff it into pastries . . . This sauce knows no bounds!

1 cup **granulated sugar**
(7.1oz / 200g)

3 tbsp **water**

6 tbsp cold **unsalted butter**
(3.2oz / 90g), cut into chunks

½ cup **heavy cream**
(4.2oz / 120g)

½ tsp **salt**

½ tsp **vanilla extract**

½ tsp **ground ginger**

½ tsp **ground green cardamom**

DIRECTIONS

1. In a medium skillet, heat the sugar and water over medium heat, stirring constantly, until the sugar is dissolved. Simmer without stirring for 4 to 5 minutes until the sugar mixture has turned golden.

2. Remove the pan from the heat. Add the cold butter and vigorously stir until the butter and sugar have combined. Return to medium heat and bring to a simmer.

3. Slowly drizzle in the heavy cream, stirring gently. Bring to a simmer.

4. Remove the pan from the heat. Add the salt, vanilla, ginger, and cardamom. Mix until combined. Let cool for a moment and transfer to a clean glass jar for storage. Refrigerate for up to 1 week.

NOTE: This caramel sauce will solidify a bit in the fridge, but all you need to get it runny is some heat—30 seconds in the microwave or submerging the sealed glass jar in hot water for a few minutes will usually do the trick!

The best dessert is no dessert. Hear me out.

I have a bit of a controversial opinion to share. It's about dessert, and you might not like it. I believe that the best dessert you can eat after a meal is no dessert. Before you get angry, hear me out!

Imagine you just finished a big dinner. It was one for the history books, with bold flavors, multiple courses, and great company—perhaps a glass or two of wine may have been involved. But we all know the saying: there is always room for dessert.

This is not just something we say; there's an actual physiological explanation—sensory overload. When exposed to something in unusually large qualities for a prolonged period of time (or deprived of something), our senses adapt. It's the reason you don't smell your apartment until you come back from vacation or start seeing better in the dark after a few minutes. A similar thing happens when you eat a meal. Since the main courses tend to be salty and savory, after a while, your body is satiated nutritionally, but that little glutton inside of you still craves the only taste it didn't get enough of: sweetness. And so you go for that apple pie, tiramisu, or pastry (which probably disappeared off your plate before you could say "chocolate cake").

In truth though, you remain in sensory overload, and this is where my controversial opinion comes in: skip the dessert. I am not saying you shouldn't have the dessert—I'm just saying don't have it *now*.

Let's first talk about that craving for a sweet treat to end the meal—I am with you. But instead of reaching for a heavy, Western-style dessert, I find myself opting for something else instead: fruit. In some of the countries I have visited where traditional food habits have been preserved and not pushed out by advancement, people will often snack from a fruit platter after a meal. This shouldn't even seem odd—fruits are, after all, nature's OG desserts. They scratch that itch when you need something sweet, but they are, objectively, the more reasonable choice.

"What about that delicious slice of banana bread, though?" you might ask. Don't worry, I don't want to deprive you. In fact, I'm on your side—I want you to get the absolute most out of it. How do you do that? By introducing more teatimes to your life. While teatime or a cultural equivalent exists almost anywhere in the world (from dim sum teahouse culture to British afternoon tea), I sometimes feel like we're not doing it enough. Unfairly so, because it could be your new favorite mealtime.

Right when you start drifting off into that late afternoon slump on a long day of working or studying, that's the golden window to have afternoon tea. It can be a quick sit-down with a friend or colleague who happens to be nearby, or even just a little self-care ritual. I would recommend actually making tea (or an herbal infusion if, like me, you tend to be quite sensitive to caffeine later in the day), putting on some music you're in the mood for, and just taking a little moment to enjoy that dessert you've been craving.

Look, you can even do this after taking a little break following your main dinner event. All I'm saying is, you'll be amazed how much more you can get out of the same dish when you consume it not in a state of sensory overload but with rested and ready-to-roll taste buds.

I'm the last person who would ever tell you to stop eating anything. But especially for the more sinful things we like to eat to stay happy, being a little more conscientious helps us to really get the most out of every calorie. And actively making dessert a teatime event is about more than just that: it can help us make those moments of indulgence more memorable. In the end, that's what is at the heart of the food I like the most: it helps me to make new memories and to experience and enjoy life more.

SUAN MEI TANG
(CHINESE SUMMER DRINK)

MAKES
Two 32-ounce (1L) bottles

PREP TIME
5 minutes + 30 minutes to steep

COOK TIME
60 minutes

This is hands-down the most refreshing drink I've ever had and about the only thing that can cool me down on a blistering summer day. The ingredient list may be intimidating, but if you're up for a unique flavor experience and a drink you are not likely to encounter anywhere else, this is for you.

DIRECTIONS

1. In a mesh sieve, rinse the plums, hawthorn, orange peel, and licorice root to remove impurities and dust. Add to a large pot along with the hibiscus flower and water. Let soak for 30 minutes at room temperature.

2. Bring to a boil over high heat, then reduce the heat to low, cover, and simmer for 45 minutes. Add water if necessary to maintain a consistent water level.

3. Add the sugar, osmanthus flower, and mint. Simmer for 10 more minutes.

4. Using a fine mesh sieve, strain the tea of its solids and bottle it. Chill in the fridge or serve in a glass with ice.

NOTE: If you're unable to find smoked dried plums, you can use dried apricots or salted ume instead.

2 oz (60g) **smoked dried plums** (see note)

3 oz (85g) **dried hawthorn**

¼ oz (7g) **dried orange peel**

¼ oz (7g) **dried licorice root**

½ oz (15g) **dried hibiscus flower** or 2 bags **unscented fruity tea,** such as rose hip

8 cups **water** (2L)

3½ oz (100g) **brown sugar**

1 tbsp **dried osmanthus flower**

½ tbsp **dried mint**

BANANA BREAD

SERVES
4-6

PREP TIME
20 minutes

COOK TIME
1 hour 10 minutes

On my quest to find a banana bread recipe I actually like, I think I finally cracked the code. The biggest key to success? Using bananas that are not just overripe, but ones that are actually black—almost at the point of starting to go bad. Add to that some browned butter and a dash of rum, and top the loaf with chopped almonds. We've got ourselves a winner.

DIRECTIONS

1. Preheat the oven to 350°F (190°C). Grease an 8 x 4-inch (20 x 10cm) loaf pan and lightly dust with flour.

2. In a medium saucepan, heat the butter and slowly simmer over medium heat for 10 minutes or until browned but not burnt. It should give off a toasty aroma. Transfer to a medium bowl to cool.

3. In a large bowl, whisk together the flour, brown sugar (reserve 1 tablespoon), baking powder, kosher salt, and cinnamon.

4. On a plate or in a shallow bowl, mash the bananas with a fork to a smooth consistency with some chunks remaining.

5. Add the banana mash to the bowl with the cooled butter. Add the sour cream, eggs, rum, and vanilla bean. Mix until well combined.

6. Pour the wet ingredients into the bowl with the dry ingredients. Fold just until no large patches of flour remain. You will end up with a shaggy, wet batter.

7. Pour the batter into the prepared loaf pan. With a wet spatula, smooth out to level and sprinkle the top with the almonds and reserved 1 tablespoon brown sugar. Place on the middle rack and bake for 60 minutes or until the internal temperature registers at least 175°F (80°C).

8. Remove from the oven and let cool in the loaf pan for 10 minutes. Carefully transfer to a cooling rack to cool completely.

9. Slice and serve plain or with a scoop of vanilla ice cream, salted caramel sauce (page 241), or my favorite, a glass of bourbon.

NOTES: Keep the scraped out vanilla pod in a small container with sugar to make vanilla sugar for future use.

If the almonds in the topping begin to toast too quickly, cover with foil to prevent burning.

4½ oz (130g) **butter,** plus more for greasing pan

1½ cups **all-purpose flour** (6.3oz / 180g)

1 cup **brown sugar** (7.1oz / 200g), reserve 1 tbsp

2 tsp **baking powder**

½ tsp **kosher salt**

½ tsp **ground cinnamon**

2 overripe, blackened **bananas** (7.1oz / 200g)

½ cup **sour cream**

2 large **eggs**

1 tbsp **Jamaican rum** or ⅛ tsp **rum extract** (optional)

1 **vanilla bean,** seeds only (see note)

¼ cup **blanched slivered almonds** (1.8oz / 50g)

Flaky salt, to taste

CHOCOLATE "POTATOES"

MAKES
10 chocolate potatoes

PREP TIME
20 minutes

COOK TIME
None

These sweet treats are a monument to Soviet food culture and a family favorite of mine. Whenever I have relatives visiting from Russia, they are guaranteed to bring a few chocolate potatoes. The name obviously refers to the way they look, but don't be mistaken: no actual potatoes are involved. Instead, this is pure chocolatey, buttery goodness.

DIRECTIONS

1. In a food processor, process the graham crackers for 1 minute or until fully pulverized into a fine powder.

2. In a large bowl, whisk together the pulverized crackers and 2 tablespoons cocoa powder. Add the condensed milk, butter, and rum. Mix until it comes together into one smooth ball.

3. Divide the dough into 10 equally sized portions. Using your hands, form each portion into a potato shape. Work quickly to prevent the dough from melting in your hands.

4. Toss the "potatoes" in the remaining cocoa powder until covered and place on serving plates.

5. To make the buttercream, in a small bowl, combine all ingredients. Mix until the sugar is completely incorporated and the mixture is smooth and homogeneous. Transfer into a piping bag.

6. With the pointy end of a chopstick, add 4 to 6 little holes along the top of each "potato." Use the piping bag to create a row of 4 to 6 little "shoots" by piping a little bit of buttercream into each hole.

7 oz (200g) **graham crackers**

4 tbsp **Dutch-process cocoa powder** (1.4oz / 40g), divided

½ cup **sweetened condensed milk** (5.3oz / 150g)

8 tbsp **butter** (4oz / 115g), softened

1 tbsp **Jamaican rum** or ⅛ tsp **rum extract**

FOR THE BUTTERCREAM

4 tbsp **butter** (2.1oz / 60g), softened

⅓ cup **confectioners sugar** (2oz / 50g)

¼ tsp **vanilla extract**

½ tsp **lemon juice**

Acknowledgments

I never thought writing a book would be easy, but in the end it was even more challenging than I expected. I would never have been able to do it if it weren't for the many amazing people who have worked so hard to help me make it a reality!

Thank you to Kilian for spending weeks in the kitchen with me developing and testing recipes. And thank you to all the friends and studio guests who helped me taste and evaluate the many batches it took, not all of which I would describe as enjoyable.

Thank you to Eypee, Diana, Jana, and Sissi for making the recipes come to life in the most beautiful way. Our two-week photo shoot was one of the most fun projects I've ever gotten to do. Thank you to Vic for the great times we had shooting the book cover and running around Berlin snapping pictures of me!

Thank you to Grace for having my back throughout the entire project. You were the second pair of hands and eyes I needed; without you I would never have been able to go through with this massive undertaking.

Thank you to Ann for being so patient with me as I stumbled through the process of putting together an actual cookbook for the very first time. Thank you to Lovoni for double-checking every single recipe, and thank you to Jessica for making everything come together so beautifully! All of you are real pros, and your guidance was indispensable.

Last but not least, thank you to my family for being so incredibly supportive. Mom, Greg, Tata, Enna, Shurik—you all helped in every way you could, and I am eternally grateful for that! ♥

About the Author

Arseny Knaifel (aka **Andong**) is a Berlin-based YouTuber, filmmaker, chef, and podcaster. His work revolves around exploring the origins and stories behind the foods that move the world. Whether it's your favorite supermarket snack, a little-known local specialty only found off the beaten travel paths, or a much-loved street-food classic, Andong will cook and eat them all, and share them with his global audience of over a half-million passionate foodies.

Index

A

agave syrup, 15

Andean Green Salsa, 74

Anti-Perfectionist Pad Thai, 111

Avocado & Tomato Salad, 153

B

Baba Ganoush, 120

bamboo steamer, 13

Banana Bread, 247

Bavarian Cheese Spread
(Obazda), 213

beef
Beef Burgundy, 181
Beef, Celery & Carrot Filling (jiaozi),
71
Lomo Saltado (Peruvian Stir-Fry),
195
Easy Plov (Uzbek Rice Pilaf), 191
Spicy Beef Crumble Topping
(hummus), 131
Uzbek-Style Beef Filling (samosas),
82

Beet Salad (Russian Vinegret), 159

Berlin-Style döner kebab, 92
Berlin-Style Chicken Döner Kebab,
95
Döner Bread, 97
Döner Sauce, 96

Better Than Fanta, 237

Black Bean Ful Medames, 24

Blini (Russian Pancakes), 35

Bolivian Hand Pies (Salteñas),
72–73

borscht, 40
Souped Up Borscht, 44
Svekolnik (Summer Borscht), 45

Bourdain, Anthony, 8

breakfast, 16–37
Black Bean Ful Medames, 24

Blini (Russian Pancakes), 35
Chechebsa (Ethiopian Spiced
Honey Flatbread), 33
Chicken Congee, 21
Chilaquiles, 27
Chinese breakfast, 18
crullers, 18, 23
Pandesal (Filipino Sweet Milk Buns),
31
Jian Bing (Chinese Breakfast
Crepe), 37
porridge, 18
Russian blini, 19
Youtiao, 23
zhou, 18

Burmese salads, 148
Avocado & Tomato Salad, 153
Tea Leaf Coleslaw, 152

C

Cabbage & Egg Filling (pirozhki),
89

Canh Chua, Grace's (Vietnamese
Sweet & Sour Soup), 47

Causa (Peruvian Layered Potato
Salad), 163

Chechebsa (Ethiopian Spiced
Honey Flatbread), 33

cheese
Blini (Russian Pancakes), 35
Cuban Sandwich, Germanized, 115
Fusion Cheesy Garlic Noodles, 134
Obazda (Bavarian Cheese Spread),
213

chicken
Causa (Peruvian Layered Potato
Salad), 163
Chicken Adobo with Garlic Rice,
187
Chicken Congee, 21
Chicken Filling (pirozhki), 89
Coca-Cola Chicken Wings, 133
Gu Lou Yuk (Hong Kong–Style

Sweet & Sour Chicken), 193
Hainanese Chicken Rice, 178–179
Peking Duck Chicken Wraps, 197
Salteñas (Bolivian Hand Pies),
72–73
Shrimp Balls, 51

chilaquiles, 18
Chilaquiles, 27

chili crisp, 200
Chili Crisp, 204

chimichurri, 200
Chimichurri, 221

Chinese Breakfast Crepe (Jian
Bing), 37

Chinese cold dishes, 148

Chinese dumplings, 63

Chinese Summer Drink (Suan Mei
Tang), 245

Chinese Tofu, Celery & Carrot
Salad (Three-Sliver Salad), 168

Chinese turnip cake, 121
Chinese Turnip Cake (Lou Bo Gao),
138–139

Chiu Chow Chili Oil, 205, 217

Chocolate "Potatoes," 249

Chow Mein, Forbidden, 117

Churros, 235

Chutagi (Ladakhi Noodle Stew),
125

chutneys, 200
Green Chutney, 210
Red Chutney, 211

citric acid, 15

citrus zest, dried, 14

clarified butter/ghee, 14

Clear Hot Pot Broth Base (Vegan),
184

Coca-Cola Chicken Wings, 133

coffee, instant, 15

Cold Summer Borscht (Svekolnik), 45

condiments. *See* sauces and condiments

cornstarch, 14

crepes
Blini (Russian Pancakes), 35
Jian Bing (Chinese Breakfast Crepe), 37

crullers, 18, 23
Youtiao (Chinese Breakfast Cruller), 23

Cuban Sandwich, Germanized, 115

cutting boards, 13

D

desserts, 228–249
Banana Bread, 247
Churros, 235
Dulce de Leche, Easy Mode, 240
Chocolate "Potatoes," 249
Russian Syrniki Muffins, 233
Salted Caramel Sauce, 241

dim sum, 121

dinner, 172–197
Beef Burgundy, 181
Chicken Adobo with Garlic Rice, 187
Clear Hot Pot Broth Base (Vegan), 184
Easy Plov (Uzbek Rice Pilaf), 191
Gu Lou Yuk (Hong Kong–Style Sweet & Sour Chicken), 193
Hainanese Chicken Rice, 178–179
Hot Pot Add-Ins, 184
Hot Pot Dipping Sauce, 185
Lomo Saltado (Peruvian Stir-Fry), 195
Peking Duck Chicken Wrap, 174, 197
Sichuan-Style Hot Pot Base Broth, 182

Döner Bread (döner kebab), 97

Döner Kebab, Chicken 95

döner kebab, story of, 108–109

Döner Sauce (döner kebab), 96

dough scraper, 12

dried citrus zest, 14

dulce de leche, 231
Dulce de Leche, Easy Mode, 240

dumplings, 60–89
Beef, Celery & Carrot Filling (jiaozi), 71
Bolivian Salteñas, 72–73
Cabbage & Egg Filling (pirozhki), 89
Chicken Filling (pirozhki), 89
Chinese dumplings, 63
Jiaozi, 68
Kuya Eypee's Lumpia (Filipino-Style Spring Rolls), 64
lumpia shanghai, 62
making (as group activity), 78
Momdong's Russian Pirozhki, 86
Oven-Baked Samosas, 80
Pork & Bok Choy Filling (jiaozi), 71
Pork & Shrimp Filling (lumpia), 67
Pork & Shrimp Wontons with Chili Oil, 85
Potato Masala Filling (samosas), 82
Russian pirozhki, 62
samosas, 63
Sheng Jian Bao, 76
Tofu & Mushroom Filling (lumpia), 67
Uzbek-Style Beef Filling (samosas), 82
wontons, 62

E

Easy Hummus with Toppings, 129
Feta, Mango, & Chili Topping, 130
Smoky Paprika Yogurt Topping, 130
Spicy Beef Crumble Topping, 131
Zesty Pesto Topping, 131

Easy Plov (Uzbek Rice Pilaf), 191

Easy Rempah (Red Curry Paste), 50

eggplant
Baba Ganoush, 123
Uzbek Eggplant Salad, 155

eggs
Cabbage & Egg Filling (pirozhki), 89
Chilaquiles, 27
Tomato Fried Eggs, 145

equipment. *See* tools

Ethiopian Spiced Honey Flatbread (Chechebsa), 33

F

Falafel Fried Rice, 141

Fanta, Better Than, 237

Fattoush, 165

Feta, Mango & Chili Topping (hummus), 130

Filipino Sweet Milk Buns (Pandesal), 31

Filipino-Style Spring Rolls (lumpia), 64

five spice powder, 15

Flammkuchen, 113

flatbread, 18
Chechebsa (Ethiopian Spiced Honey Flatbread), 33

Forbidden Chow Mein, 117

Ful Medames, Black Bean, 24

Fusion Cheesy Garlic Noodles, 134

G

garlic powder, 14

German Potato Salad, 157

ghee, 14

Ginger Scallion Crisp, 223

Grace's Canh Chua (Vietnamese Sweet & Sour Soup), 47

grater, 13

Green Chutney, 210

Gu Lou Yuk (Hong Kong–Style Sweet & Sour Chicken), 193

H–I

Hainanese chicken rice, 174, 188–189
    Hainanese Chicken Rice, 178–179

Hand-Pulled Noodles with Chili Soy Dressing, 127

Hong Kong–Style Sweet & Sour Chicken (Gu Lou Yuk), 193

hot pot, 175
    Clear Hot Pot Broth Base (Vegan), 184
    Hot Pot Add-Ins, 184
    Hot Pot Dipping Sauce, 185
    Sichuan-Style Hot Pot Base Broth, 182

hummus, 120
    Easy Hummus with Toppings, 129
    Feta, Mango & Chili Topping, 130
    Smoky Paprika Yogurt Topping, 130
    Spicy Beef Crumble Topping, 131
    Zesty Pesto Topping, 131

instant coffee, 15

J

Jian Bing (Chinese Breakfast Crepe), 37

jiaozi, 62
    Beef, Celery & Carrot Filling, 71
    Jiaozi, 68
    Pork & Bok Choy Filling, 71

K

kalitki, 93
    Karelian Kalitki, 98

Karelian Kalitki, 98

Potato Filling, 101

Salmon Filling, 100

kebab, Berlin-Style Chicken Döner Kebab, 95

kitchen torch, 13

knives, 12

Kuya Eypee's Lumpia (Filipino-Style Spring Rolls), 64
    Pork & Shrimp Filling, 67
    Tofu & Mushroom Filling, 67

Kuya Rafa's Sawsawan Dip, 215

L

Ladakhi Noodle Stew (Chutagi), 125

lahpet thoke, 152

Laksa, Tom Kha Style, 48

lentils, Turkish Lentil Soup, 59

liang cai, 148

Lohikeitto, 55

Lomo Saltado (Peruvian Stri-Fry), 195

Lou Bo Gao (Chinese Turnip Cake), 138–139

lumpia shanghai, 62
    Kuya Eypee's Lumpia (Filipino-Style Spring Rolls), 64
    Pork & Shrimp Filling, 67
    Tofu & Mushroom Filling, 67

lunch. *See* midday meals

M

mayonnaise, 14

mercimek çorbası (Turkish lentil soup), 40
    Turkish Lentil Soup, 59

midday meals, 118–145
    Baba Ganoush, 123
    Chinese Turnip Cake (Lou Bo Gao), 138–139
    Chutagi (Ladakhi Noodle Stew), 125
    Coca-Cola Chicken Wings, 133

dim sum, 121

Easy Hummus with Toppings, 129

Falafel Fried Rice, 141

Feta, Mango & Chili Topping (hummus), 130

Fusion Cheesy Garlic Noodles, 134

Hand-Pulled Noodles with Chili Soy Dressing, 127

hummus, 120

Levantine cuisine, 120

Pasta e Fagioli, 142

rice, 121

Smoky Paprika Yogurt Topping (hummus), 130

Spicy Beef Crumble Topping (hummus), 131

Tomato Fried Eggs, 145

Zesty Pesto Topping (hummus), 131

milk powder, 15

Momdong's Russian Pirozhki, 86
    Cabbage & Egg Filling, 89
    Chicken Filling, 89

mortar and pestle, 12

MSG, 11

mushrooms
    Beef Burgundy, 181
    Sichuan-Style Black Wood Ear Mushrooms, 171
    Tofu & Mushroom Filling (lumpia), 67

N

noodles
    Anti-Perfectionist Pad Thai, 111
    Chutagi (Ladakhi Noodle Stew), 125
    Fusion Cheesy Garlic Noodles, 134
    Hand-Pulled Noodles with Chili Soy Dressing, 127
    Laksa, Tom Kha Style, 48

O

Obazda (Bavarian Cheese Spread), 213

onion powder, 14

Oven-Baked Samosas, 80

Potato Masala Filling, 82

Uzbek-Style Beef Filling, 82

P–Q

pad thai, 93

Anti-Perfectionist Pad Thai, 111

Pandesal (Filipino Sweet Milk Buns), 31

pantry, 14–15

agave syrup, 15

citric acid, 15

citrus zest, dried, 14

clarified butter/ghee, 14

cornstarch, 14

dried citrus zest, 14

garlic powder, 14

instant coffee, 15

mayonnaise, 14

milk powder, 15

onion powder, 14

spice blends, 15

tahini, 14

toasted sesame seeds, 15

panzanella, 165

Pasta e Fagioli, 142

Peking Duck Chicken Wraps, 174, 197

Peruvian Layered Potato Salad (Causa), 163

pickles, Semi-Salted Dill Pickles, 226

pirozhki, Momdong's Russian Pirozhki, 86

plov, 175

Easy Plov (Uzbek Rice Pilaf), 191

pork

Pork & Bok Choy Filling (jiaozi), 71

Pork & Shrimp Filling (lumpia), 67

Pork & Shrimp Wontons with Chili Oil, 85

porridge, 18

Chicken Congee, 21

potatoes, 149

Causa (Peruvian Layered Potato Salad), 163

German Potato Salad, 157

Potato Filling (kalitki), 101

Potato Masala Filling (samosas), 82

Pretzels, 103

R

Red Chutney, 211

rempah spice paste, 41

Easy Rempah (Red Curry Paste), 50

rice, 121

Chicken Adobo with Garlic Rice, 187

Chicken Congee, 21

Falafel Fried Rice, 141

Hainanese Chicken Rice, 178–179

Easy Plov (Uzbek Rice Pilaf), 191

Russian blini, 19

Blini (Russian Pancakes), 35

Russian pirozhki, 62

Cabbage & Egg Filling, 89

Chicken Filling, 89

Momdong's Russian Pirozhki, 86

Russian Sauerkraut, 227

Russian semi-salted pickles, 201

Russian Syrniki Muffins, 233

Russian Vinegret (Beet Salad), 159

S

salads, 146–171

Avocado & Tomato Salad, 153

Causa (Peruvian Layered Potato Salad), 163

Chinese cold dishes, 148

enigma of, 160

Fattoush, 165

German Potato Salad, 157

lahpet thoke, 152

liang cai, 148

panzanella, 165

Russian Vinegret (Beet Salad), 159

Sichuan-Style Black Wood Ear Mushrooms, 171

Tangy Spinach and Peanut Salad, 169

Tea Leaf Coleslaw, 152

thoke, 148

Three-Sliver Salad (Chinese Tofu, Celery & Carrot Salad), 168

Uzbek Eggplant Salad, 155

Vinegret, 149

Salmon Filling (kalitki), 100

salsa, Andean Green Salsa, 74

Salted Caramel Sauce, 241

Salteñas (Bolivian Hand Pies), 72–73

samosas, 63

Oven-Baked Samosas, 80

Potato Masala Filling (samosas), 82

Uzbek-Style Beef Filling (samosas), 82

sauces and condiments, 198–227

Chili Crisp, 204

Chimichurri, 221

Chiu Chow Chili Oil, 205, 217

chutneys, 200

Ginger Scallion Crisp, 223

Green Chutney, 210

Kuya Rafa's Sawsawan Dip, 215

Obazda (Bavarian Cheese Spread), 213

Red Chutney, 211

Russian Sauerkraut, 227

Russian semi-salted pickles, 201

Semi-Salted Dill Pickles, 226

Svanetian Salt, 218

Sweet Chili Sauce, 207

Scallion Pancakes, 104

scissors, 12

Semi-Salted Dill Pickles, 226

sesame seeds, toasted, 15

sheng jian bao, 63

Sheng Jian Bao, 76

shrimp

Pork & Shrimp Wontons with Chili Oil, 85

Shrimp Balls, 51

Sichuan-Style Black Wood Ear Mushrooms, 171

Sichuan-Style Hot Pot Base Broth, 182

silicone spatulas, 12

Smoky Paprika Yogurt Topping (hummus), 130

soups, 38–59
Souped Up Borscht, 44
Grace's Canh Chua (Vietnamese Sweet & Sour Soup), 47
Easy Rempah (Red Curry Paste), 50
history, 52–53
Laksa, Tom Kha Style, 48
Lohikeitto, 55
mercimek çorbası (Turkish lentil soup), 40
Shrimp Balls, 51
Svekolnik (Cold Summer Borscht), 45
Turkish Lentil Soup, 59
West African Peanut Soup, 56

sparkling water, 230

spatulas, silicone, 12

spice blends, 15

Spicy Beef Crumble Topping (hummus), 131

steamer, bamboo, 13

storytelling in food, value of, 11

straining utensils, 12

street food, 90–117
Anti-Perfectionist Pad Thai, 111
Berlin-Style Chicken Döner Kebab, 95
chow mein, 93
Cuban Sandwich, Germanized, 115
Döner Bread (döner kebab), 97
döner kebab, story of, 108–109
Döner Sauce (döner kebab), 96
Flammkuchen, 113
Forbidden Chow Mein, 117
Karelian Kalitki, 98
pad thai, 93
Potato Filling (kalitki), 101
Pretzels, 103
Salmon Filling (kalitki), 100
Scallion Pancakes, 104

suan mei tang, 230
Suan Mei Tang (Chinese Summer Drink), 245

summer borscht, 40
Svekolnik (Cold Summer Borscht), 45

Svanetian salt, 201
Svanetian Salt, 218

Svekolnik (Cold Summer Borscht), 45

Sweet Chili Sauce, 207

syrniki, 231
Russian Syrniki Muffins, 233

T

tahini, 14

Tangy Spinach and Peanut Salad, 169

Tea Leaf Coleslaw, 152

thoke, 148

Three-Sliver Salad (Chinese Tofu, Celery & Carrot Salad), 168

toasted sesame seeds, 15

tofu
Three-Sliver Salad (Chinese Tofu, Celery & Carrot Salad), 168
Tofu & Mushroom Filling (lumpia), 67

tomato fried eggs, 121
Tomato Fried Eggs, 145

tools, 12–13
bamboo steamer, 13
cutting boards, 13
dough scraper, 12
grater, 13
kitchen scale, 12
kitchen torch, 13
knives, 12
large bowls, 13
mortar and pestle, 12
scissors, 12
silicone spatulas, 12
straining utensils, 12
wok, 13

torch, kitchen, 13

Turkish Lentil Soup, 59

U–V

Uzbek eggplant salad, 148
Uzbek Eggplant Salad, 155

Uzbek-Style Beef Filling (samosas), 82

Vietnamese Sweet & Sour Soup (Grace's Canh Chua), 47

Vinegret, Russian, 159

W–X

West African Peanut Soup, 56

wok, 13

wontons, 62
Pork & Shrimp Wontons with Chili Oil, 85

Y–Z

Youtiao, 23

Zesty Pesto Topping (hummus), 131

zhou, 18